T0304954

'Carol Gray's Social Stories™ are known to virtually everyone associated with Autism Spectrum Disorders. In this new book, Siobhan Timmins, parent of a child with ASD who studied under Carol Gray, helps to further explain Gray's Social Stories™ as a way of assisting children with ASD to control behaviors and function at a higher level. The book gives a clear, detailed, and thoughtful explanation of the central ideas behind Social Stories™ and demonstrates how to implement the strategies with wonderful examples and terrific pictures. Anyone interested in the ideas and strategies behind Social Stories™ will love this clear and in depth elaboration of the theories and practices and the delightful examples of how to implement them.'

– Gary B. Mesibov, Professor Emeritus of Psychology and Emeritus Research Fellow at the University of North Carolina at Chapel Hill

'This book is an invaluable contribution to the body of published information and guidance on Carol Gray's Social Stories™. Siobhan shares her insightful thinking and information gathering which results in impeccable stories for her son Mark. Her stories and the strategies she uses to ensure true social understanding will be inspirational to all parents and professionals.'

– Eileen Arnold, former specialist speech and language therapist and co-author of Revealing the Hidden Social Code: Social Stories™ for People with Autistic Spectrum Disorders

of related interest

My Social Stories™ Book
Edited by Carol Gray and Abbie Leigh White
Illustrated by Sean McAndrew
ISBN 978 1 85302 950 9
eISBN 978 0 85700 166 5

Revealing the Hidden Social Code
Social Stories™ for People with Autistic Spectrum Disorders
Marie Howley and Eileen Arnold
ISBN 978 1 84310 222 9
eISBN 978 1 84642 142 6

What Did You Say? What Do You Mean?
Jude Welton
Illustrated by Jane Telford
ISBN 9781843102076
eISBN 9781846424380

Can I Tell You About Asperger Syndrome?
A Guide for Friends and Family
Jude Welton
Illustrated by Jane Telford
ISBN 9781843102069
eISBN 9781846424229

Can I Tell You about Autism?
A Guide for Friends, Family and Professionals
Jude Welton
Illustrated by Jane Telford
ISBN 9781849054539
eISBN 9780857008299

SUCCESSFUL SOCIAL STORIES™ FOR YOUNG CHILDREN

GROWING UP WITH SOCIAL STORIES™

SIOBHAN TIMMINS
FOREWORD BY CAROL GRAY

Jessica Kingsley *Publishers*
London and Philadelphia

First published in 2016
by Jessica Kingsley Publishers
73 Collier Street
London N1 9BE, UK
and
400 Market Street, Suite 400
Philadelphia, PA 19106, USA

www.jkp.com

Copyright © Siobhan Timmins 2016
Foreword copyright © Carol Gray 2016

All rights reserved. No part of this publication may be reproduced in any material
form (including photocopying or storing it in any medium by electronic means and
whether or not transiently or incidentally to some other use of this publication)
without the written permission of the copyright owner except in accordance with the
provisions of the Copyright, Designs and Patents Act 1988 or under the terms of a
licence issued by the Copyright Licensing Agency Ltd, Saffron House, 6–10 Kirby
Street, London EC1N 8TS. Applications for the copyright owner's written permission
to reproduce any part of this publication should be addressed to the publisher.

Warning: The doing of an unauthorised act in relation to a copyright work
may result in both a civil claim for damages and criminal prosecution.

Library of Congress Cataloging in Publication Data
Names: Timmins, Siobhan, author.
Title: Successful social stories for young children / Siobhan Timmins ;
   foreword by Carol Gray.
Description: Philadelphia : Jessica Kingsley Publishers, 2016. | Includes
   bibliographical references.
Identifiers: LCCN 2016010705 | ISBN 9781785921124 (alk. paper)
Subjects: LCSH: Self-control in children. | Social perception in children. |
   Social learning. | Life skills. | Autistic children.
Classification: LCC BF723.S25 T56 2016 | DDC 155.4/192--dc23 LC record available
at https://urldefense.proofpoint.com/v2/url?u=https-3A__lccn.loc.gov_2016010705&
d=BQIFAg&c=euGZstcaTDllvimEN8b7jXrwqOf-v5A_CdpgnVfiiMM&r=jDhEGalRB
ceh95Jy341lNgmWR9tnCifzbrA2NWHfaH8&m=G-jSyAkwCW8fUZRsLesTT3BEzEh
OtLQF416fZj0e6LA&s=drzDAvnAzsRJBmSzme9shQDZxB21Uuy2frs2fU26lMQ&e

British Library Cataloguing in Publication Data
A CIP catalogue record for this book is available from the British Library

ISBN 978 1 78592 112 4
eISBN 978 1 78450 376 5

Printed and bound in Great Britain

MIX
Paper from
responsible sources
FSC® C013604

This book is dedicated to my son Mark,
who faces all challenges with
an honesty, courage and dignity
that humbles me daily.

He is my inspiration.

Contents

Foreword by Carol Gray   9

Acknowledgements   *15*

Introduction   17

Understanding my child's perspective   22

What does growing up mean?   28

Stories about calm   35

I am learning to listen   51

I am learning to wait patiently   56

What are kind words?   61

What is taking turns? I am learning to share toys   66

What is a conversation?   78

How to interrupt a conversation   85

What are good manners?   91

What are table manners?   95

What does 'excuse me' mean?   102

Why do I write thank you letters?   111

I am learning to use a hand dryer   118

How to find another favourite food   126

What is my underpants' job?   134

Stories about toileting   140

What job does my nose do?   153

How to stay safe and comfy in a supermarket   161

Why do babies cry?   175

How to stay safe around wasps   182

Sharing the diagnosis with a Social Story™   193

A Story for parents at L.A.S.T.!   204

A Story for siblings   207

References   *211*

Index   *213*

Foreword

Early in 1994, Mark Timmins was diagnosed with autism. He was 2 years old. His mother, Siobhan, left her practice as a physician to read more about autism and how to best help her son. She learned about Social Stories™ at a conference, and soon after attended a Social Story™ training. To keep abreast of new developments, Siobhan returned to the annual workshops several times. All the while, she was writing for her son. In this first book of a three-volume series, *Successful Social Stories™ For Young Children: Growing Up With Social Stories™,* Siobhan shares her experiences and insights along with Mark's earliest Stories. As the person who developed Social Stories™, it is my honour to introduce you to Social Stories™, Dr. Siobhan Timmins and what makes this unprecedented book so valuable to those of us working with children, adolescents and adults with autism today.

It's okay if you are not familiar with Social Stories™. Siobhan will aptly describe them on the following pages. Until then, all that you need is an introductory understanding of Social Stories™. For that, we'll start with Haikus. Haiku is a Japanese form of poetry governed by rules of format. In a Haiku, for example, seventeen syllables are divided among three lines of five, seven, and five syllables respectively, with the inclusion of at least one seasonal reference. If an author doesn't follow the rules, it's not a Haiku.

Similarly, Social Stories™ are a defined type of story. For this reason, the term *Social Story™* is always capitalised, as is *Story* when used in reference to a Social Story™. Each Story shares information via a format that is most likely to be understood by someone with autism. As with Haikus, authors of Social Stories™ follow rules, referred to as *criteria* or *defining characteristics*. Deviating from the format may result in a story, but it is not a Social Story™. Every Social Story™ has distinguishing characteristics that work to enhance meaning and, most importantly, safety for people with autism.

For many parents, the effort to become an informed and effective parent of a child with autism in the early 1990s led to more confusion and self-doubt than assurance and confidence. In 1994, the year that Siobhan's son, Mark, was diagnosed, I was an educational consultant for children with autism. I remember parents describing the search for answers as overwhelming and exhausting. That was my experience as well. Widespread use of the Internet was a few years away. Parents encountered a relatively new field, a jungle of research, ideas, trends, and conflicting opinion. Good intentions were at risk of embracing new ideas without any pre-requisite filters, 'interviews' or evaluation. It was an unbridled intentness that often translated into 'zigzag' educational programming, with valuable time consumed by trend and indecision.

Enter Dr Siobhan Timmins, a mother intriguingly well equipped to chart a path through the confusing jungle of autism information. Her goal is simple: to find strategies to help Mark that will work within her family. Siobhan is a new sort of explorer. She maintains a soft-spoken confidence that considers obstacles and opposing opinions as opportunities. In fact, Siobhan regards the entire jungle that way. No mosquito repellant needed, just information about mosquitoes is all that is required.

First and foremost, autism has no argument with Siobhan because she knows that it is not seeking one. Autism is a part of her son's profile, worthy of her respect and careful consideration. Siobhan knows that comfort is key to Mark's learning and progress. Same as it is for each of us. Any jungle vines that threaten to obstruct her vision or cause misinterpretation yield to her patient acceptance. When something is confusing, Siobhan stops and gathers information, consulting with Mark, his autism, and her observations until the path clears. It makes her an amazing author of Social Stories™.

Siobhan is extraordinary. First, just between you and me, maybe this is what happens when someone repeatedly attends a Social Story™ workshop! Information becomes protocol. Siobhan abides by the Social Story™ rules to the letter. In line with her medical training as a physician, she respects the three-step science of Social Stories™: Abandon assumptions. Gather information. Carefully develop and implement each Story. It's as if she is following an internalised and dependable pattern, a prescription that helps her determine a route to the best possible outcome.

In addition to science, there's also an art to writing Social Stories™. Internalising the rules places Siobhan in a unique position to push the lines and illustrations of Social Stories™ to the farthest margins of their potential. They are Stories written by a physician, yes, but with a mother's awareness of all that is at stake, and creativity and determination that expects each Story to work hard and 'get it right'.

Alongside Siobhan's high expectations is a 'sense' for those Stories that have the most challenging assignments; the ones that may need a little help to complete their mission honourably. Beyond basic Social Story™ science or art is Siobhan's museum quality effort to build meaning and understanding into a literary masterpiece. Here is where she excels, with ingeniously personalised 'trademark' Stories. You'll be able to identify them as you read Siobhan's descriptions that explain what she did, and why. When you find yourself thinking, 'That's GENIUS!' you're about to read a Museum Story. And, yes, it is genius. Simple. Logical. Genius.

Over the years, I've frequently referred to *The Social Story*™ *Museum* in my presentations and workshops. It's not a real place. If it was, Siobhan has enough Stories to fill an entire wing! Museum quality Stories are rare. They go beyond what is required, incorporate additional activities or materials, and as time passes, they 'stand out' in our memory.

The process of developing a Social Story™ begins with collecting relevant information. Siobhan not only *seeks* information, she often *creates* it with planned experiences for Mark. For example, after receiving a disappointing gift, Mark could not understand why he was expected to write a thank you note. In addition to gathering the standard information for the Story, Siobhan and Mark selected, purchased, wrapped, and sent a gift to a friend so that he would know first hand the effort behind a wrapped gift. The Story, *'Why do I write thank you letters?'* describes his recent shopping and sending experience, all to help Mark understand why people express appreciation in response to any gift, whether it's perfect or not quite right. As Siobhan describes, the Story '…had an immediate impact and he (Mark) was happy to write a very brief thank you letter for his disappointing birthday gift…' (paraphrased). She did the same in creating pre-requisite experiences for her Stories about air hand dryers and the role of underpants. Siobhan is the hands-down master of museum quality groundwork resulting in Stories with immediate and positive results.

I suggest that in place of reading this book, you work through it as though you have enrolled in a personalised course of study. In many of Siobhan's descriptions, there are situations that you will recognise, coupled with detailed insights and unexpected perspectives.

You may find that, with minimal or no revision, Mark's Stories also work for those in your care. Use the Stories, as well as taking advantage of the bigger learning opportunity that lies between the front and back cover.

Create and structure your own activities to internalise the information in this book. Pay close attention to Siobhan's descriptions of the events that led to each of Mark's Stories. Think about how you might develop that Story, the elements it would contain, and write it. When finished, compare it to Siobhan's Story that follows. Make note of how Siobhan enhances Story information with materials and activities that…'Just make sense.' If possible, attend a genuine Social Story™ workshop (look for the official Social Story™ logo on promotion materials). And, if you can't attend a Social Story™ workshop *each year*, as Siobhan did, just read this book three times instead! Make this information yours and use it to benefit others.

There's also something more, whether you are a parent of a child with autism, a professional, or both. Whatever your programming choices in the years to come, Siobhan's work will help you stay the course through the studies, discussions and distractions of autism. Acknowledging the value of research and the exploration of new theories and ideas, Siobhan shows us how to stay curious and current without creating a rocky and indecisive road for people who are growing up with autism. As you read this book, whatever is going on 'out there' in the field of autism will fade to the background. Siobhan's sense of assurance and unassuming focus on her son clears the 'dust' for all of us so that we can see the task at hand.

Successful Social Stories™ for Young Children: Growing Up with Social Stories™, is the very first 'life' collection of Social Stories™, a *demonstration* of what love, words, and illustrations can do when systematically put to work on behalf of a child over time. It's incredible and highly credible. I confidently leave you in the hands of a physician who became a mom of a boy with autism, and one of the most talented Social Story™ authors in the world.

Carol Gray, Social Stories™ Founder and Author
The New Social Story™ Book: Revised and
Expanded 15th Anniversary Edition
www.CarolGraySocialStories.com

Acknowledgements

First of all thanks must go to Mark for giving me permission to publish his Stories in order to help other children.

I would like to thank my mother and father, who just understood, loved and helped, and who I miss every day. Thanks too to Viv Kernick, who helped me give the boys all the time and loving attention they needed in those early years and continues to this day to be a cherished family friend. Thanks also to Helen Barker, who came into Mark's life later when he first integrated into mainstream education. Helen supported him through mainstream primary and secondary school as his learning support assistant and was his faithful guide, providing consistent understanding in every unexpected challenging situation, for 11 years. Helen too remains a close friend and an important part of our family.

Special thanks must go to Carol Gray who brought clarity to my confusion with her explanation of social understanding and changed all our lives for the better with her amazing technique of Social Stories™. Carol first suggested I put my Stories into a book and has been a source of continual support and encouragement along the way to publication.

I would like to thank Sue Anderton, founder of the MAZE programme, who supported me in my application to become a Social Stories™ Trainer and Eileen Arnold, my mentor, who set up the Social Stories™ Satellite, guided me as a trainer and encouraged me to publish.

Many thanks also go to the headmaster of Market Field School, Gary Smith, who facilitated Market Field School becoming the Social Stories™ Satellite Service for Essex and for his continual support of the Social Story™ workshops.

Thanks too to Jessica Kingsley, Emily Gowers and the team for being so enthusiastic and helpful in the publication of this book.

Most of all I must thank my sons, Mark's brothers, who have helped me by simply being themselves, and growing into the wonderful young men I always knew they would be, and my husband, whose continual love and support underpins absolutely everything I do. Thank you.

Introduction

I am the mother of three wonderful sons. When my middle son Mark was diagnosed with autism, aged 2 years, I left my work as a medical doctor to pursue strategies that would help him, and which could easily be implemented within our family life. I actively researched what was known about autism, reading books and articles, and attending many conferences to learn as much as I could.

I was tremendously fortunate to attend a Future Horizons conference in 1997, where I heard Carol Gray speak about Social Understanding and the strategy of Social Stories™. I was totally inspired by Carol's insight into how a child with autism perceives the world, and blown away by her genuine love and respect for people with autism.

I attended several workshops with Carol and began to use this strategy with amazing results. I brought my husband and later on Mark's teaching assistant, Helen Barker, to learn the technique from Carol too. Soon Mark was surrounded by people who understood his perspective and were proficient in writing Social Stories™. All members of his immediate family 'team' were empowered to help him face challenges that had seemed overwhelming before.

This wonderful tool has had a profound affect not just on Mark but on my family and me too. In order to write a Social Story™ the author needs first to have an understanding of the child's perspective in that situation. Continually writing stories allowed us to develop a deeper understanding of Mark's perspective on the world, as well as giving him a better understanding of our perspective on the world. This improved mutual understanding has changed all our lives for the better. It has changed how we communicate with each other and how we anticipate possible difficulties in new situations. Personally speaking it has broadened my mind to many different perspectives on life, which I believe has deeply enriched my life. Mark is now 24 years old and Social Articles, the more adult form of Social Stories™, continue to be an effective strategy in helping him.

I have collected my Stories together in a series of books. The first covers Stories written for the early years. The second covers Stories from the school years (primary, secondary and college). The final book is still evolving as I continue to write Stories for Mark about adult life.

Each Story has an introduction describing the situation Mark was in at the time, and how I researched, put together and supported the Story in a practical way. It also contains a few useful tips that I have learned along the way! The Stories all comply with the Social Story™ criteria but the illustrations are my own and most importantly although meaningful for Mark may not be for others. Learning to research and write Stories for my son has allowed me to develop a style of writing and illustration that is accessible and immediately meaningful for him. The Stories build upon each other, developing into a personalised bank of information that is always concretely available to him.

The first Stories I wrote were predominantly picture based with few words and the illustrations were all photographs. To begin with the photographs were in black and white so that colour would not confuse the context. I did not want him to understand the Story only when the situation involved Mum wearing a pink jumper! I would cut out irrelevant and confusing background detail as he tended to focus on details that were not relevant to the information in the text. This was before I had a computer so it involved photocopying the photograph in black and white and the use of scissors. I was extremely careful to photograph places so that they would be literally understood, often taking photos at unsocial times of day to eliminate confusing people from the scene!

I used Carol Gray's 'Comic Strip Conversations' technique (Gray, 1994) to explore our different perspectives and then took the basic stick men we drew together in these conversations, developing them into illustrations Mark would engage with in the Social Story™. He often described people by their hair colour and style, so these were key identification factors. As he became interested in anime cartoon characters he wanted his own hair to reflect that in his Stories and so, keen to keep him engaged, I complied. Because Mark's clothes are always a shade of blue, his favourite colour, he could quickly find himself in the Story by looking for the little guy in blue with brown anime hair. With the development of some language the Stories included more words, always carefully chosen to be within his understanding and following the Social Story™ criteria. Over time Comic Strip Conversation allowed him to continue to develop understanding about other's intentions, thoughts and feelings, and these influenced the later Stories, with illustrations including thought and speech bubbles.

I hope that parents may learn from my examples, not just the actual Story itself but also the description of how I researched the Story, identifying the information my child was missing. Identification of this information is, I believe, the most important part of writing an effective Social Story™. Many times I have written Stories that have not been effective despite adhering to all the criteria. On reflection and reevaluation I have discovered that the topic chosen was one I believed was the relevant one from my own perspective, but which turned out was not the topic that Mark needed from his perspective!

I also wanted to emphasise the importance of supporting the Story with a view to maximising comprehension. The use of concrete props, for example, the underpants on the radiator (in 'What is my underpants' job?') or the sugar-stained t-shirt and the insect repellant spray (in 'How to stay safe around wasps'), were all helpful in improving understanding. Modelling the information for him in real-world situations using information and phrases taken from the Stories has also definitely aided comprehension.

Sadly over the 20 years I have been using Social Stories™ I have noted that they are sometimes used to try to change a child's behaviour by telling the child what they are doing wrong, how bad this makes other people feel and then what they must do to make things better. At best these stories, which are not true Social Stories™, do not work because they are not sharing useful new social information with the child. At worst they damage the child's self-esteem by highlighting their mistakes. A Social Story™ will frequently change a response simply by giving the child the information they are missing, information that is instantly and innately available to the neurotypical child. It does so in a positive, gentle and reassuring way that just accurately informs. I think this is only fair.

For the past eight years I have been closely involved in the steering, development and implementation of a parent support group for parents of children with social and communication disorders called Spectrum in Colchester, Essex. Spectrum's philosophy is one of positive solutions shared between parents. At Spectrum I have shared what I know about social understanding and Social Stories™ with other parents, who have adapted them for their children with success. This led to me sharing information on

Social Understanding with professionals involved with the care of these children, both within Spectrum, and at Market Field Special School and also at other primary and secondary schools across Essex. In 2012 I was thrilled to be approved as a Satellite Trainer in Social Stories™ by Carol Gray and now train both professionals and parents in workshops, from my base at Market Field School, which is now the approved Social Stories™ Satellite School for Essex. I continue to be involved with teaching Social Understanding within Spectrum and also on a specialist parenting programme for parents of children with additional needs, MAZE, which reaches parents, and also professionals across Essex.

I would like to encourage all those who care for or teach a child with autism to learn this valuable technique and then work at it to become fluent. Social Stories™ will not cure your child of autism, nor are they the only useful strategy to implement, but they are effective, enduring and empowering to both parent and child, a powerful partner on your walk with autism and I speak from experience!

Understanding my child's perspective

Our children with autism often display responses that seem to be unexpected, unusual or challenging to people who do not have autism. Guidance is quickly forgotten and the same mistakes seem to occur again and again. This is frustrating and disappointing, and may occasionally lead some to believe that the child 'knows' what to do and is 'choosing' not to do it. The child may even be mistakenly described as non-compliant or defiant. Having an understanding of how our children with autism perceive the world can explain some of these unexpected responses. With better insight into how they think, we can see that many of their responses are the logical response to the world as they see it. Challenging responses are in many cases coping strategies, and 'inappropriate' responses may actually be completely appropriate for their perception of the situation.

Those of us without autism (neurotypicals) continually pick up information from our surroundings through our senses, and our brains instantaneously process this information to make sense of what is going on around us, identifying the essence of a situation, or context, in less than 200 milliseconds (Vermeulen, 2012). We do not have to switch these processes on, they are automatically there for us, providing us continuously and seamlessly with a social sense of our environment. Once a context has been identified, we then use it to focus only on the details that are socially relevant to that context, in preference to many other details present, in order to make social sense of a new or changing situation. Information can then be drawn from previous similar experiences stored in our memory, to instantly help us with the current situation, identifying whether it is safe or dangerous and allowing us to predict what may happen next. This enables us to be prepared for what comes next and to choose safe and effective responses. The final outcome usually is 'appropriate' language and behaviour to suit the situation. These processes operating are usually referred to as context sensitivity and central coherence.

Children with autism do not have these brain processes operating in the same way for them. They lack context sensitivity and have weak central coherence. So despite bring very able to notice details around them, they do not instantly recognise and use the context, and therefore focus on details that are socially irrelevant, but which are instead particularly interesting for them. They are therefore less able, or unable, to understand quickly what sort of social situation they are in and therefore less likely to choose a safe and effective response for that situation. Instead they choose a response that is related to the details they have focused on. They require time to consciously work out the context, time that is not available in the quick to and fro of a rapidly changing social interaction or situation.

In a similar way, children with autism often have difficulty making social sense of the clues involved in facial expressions, tone of voice and body language in other people. They may be less able to discern how these clues give an idea of the internal context of that person, and what emotion that person may be currently experiencing.

As a consequence of this difficulty with context and making sense of a social situation our children may be less able or unable to recognise when a situation is coming to an end and a new situation is beginning. Because any new situation is also difficult to make sense of, change becomes frightening and disturbing and results in huge anxiety. In order to prevent change and to relieve this anxiety our children may strive to control the people and objects in the environment and keep everything the same. They may feel reassured by structure and ritual, being soothed by repetitive activities like watching the same video clip over and over – perhaps the only time they can truly predict what is coming next.

In addition to immediately grasping the context of a situation neurotypicals are also able to make good guesses all the time about what another person may be thinking, feeling, knowing or believing. Being able to make good guesses about other people's thoughts is often referred to as having 'theory of mind', and an absence or difficulty in this area is a common feature to all those on the autistic spectrum. Having this ability allows us to be aware that we may be upsetting, annoying or boring another person, and stimulates us to stop what we are doing, change topic or move away. This keeps us safe and effective in our interactions with other people. Without this ability a child with autism will simply not have other people's thoughts and feelings in mind during his interactions with others. He may find it difficult or impossible to understand another's perspective of a situation or interaction. He may continue with a conversation for example, without taking turns to listen, oblivious to the other person's upset or boredom, or he may state a fact about another child's appearance or performance that hurts their feelings. This makes it difficult for him to make and keep friendships.

Without this ability to have in mind what other people may be thinking, feeling or needing a child with autism will most likely also have difficulty in situations where his needs are not immediately met. Being mindful of the needs and feelings of other children brings an understanding of the 'fairness' in waiting patiently for your turn. Without this information his perception may be, for example, that he needs help now and that it is being withheld from him, resulting in a frustrated response.

Children with autism may also understand language very literally or a-contextually. This means that they do not 'see' words within the context in which they are set, and therefore are unable to understand the intended meaning. So they may have difficulty understanding the meaning behind common figures of speech such as sarcasm, metaphors, similes, double negatives and rhetorical questions, which have an intended meaning led by the context that is different or even opposite to what the words actually say. Because neurotypicals can instantly read the context we know when to take a phrase literally and when not to.

For example, when a person accidentally drops and smashes a plate she may say 'Oh great!' in a sarcastic tone of voice. Because neurotypicals can read context accurately, they understand that in this context the meaning of these words must be the opposite of the usual meaning of 'great'. However, a child with autism may perceive the person as being pleased she has dropped a plate, understanding the comment a-contextually or literally. He may even copy the action and then be surprised when told off!

Negative commands are also frequently challenging for a child with autism because they require a child not only to understand what it is he is not to do, but also to know what alternative response is expected. This requires the child to recognise and use the context to make a good guess about what the teacher or parent may be thinking, feeling or expecting when she issues a negative command in this context. This is a task he is unable to do well, if at all, due to lack of context sensitivity and poor theory of mind.

For example, when a teacher points along a corridor and instructs the children standing in line beside her 'Don't run down the corridor!' a neurotypical child, using his ability to read context and theory of mind, guesses immediately what the teacher wants him to do in this situation and walks down the corridor. A child with autism may be less able or unable to make a good guess about either what the context is or what the adult is thinking and expecting. He may be confused by the command and signal and so may stand still, appearing less compliant or even defiant. The use of positive language in communicating with children with autism prevents this confusion. Directing the children to 'Walk down the corridor' would, more likely than not, have resulted in a compliant response.

Children with autism are subjected to a large amount of negative language in their day-to-day life. They may struggle to maintain self-esteem as a result. The use of positive language, in written or verbal communication, not only improves their comprehension but also helps their self-esteem.

It is very clear that children with autism have a different perspective of the world to their neurotypical peers and their responses may seem unusual to us because of this difference. It is important to accept that their perspective is as valid to them as ours is to us. We need to respect this difference, find the missing information and share it with them. Once this is done two extraordinary things happen. First, nine times out of ten, their response changes as they have a new understanding of the situation, which they were unable to access before. Second, the more we strive to understand their perspective the more we come to see that nearly all their responses are just that – responses to a stimulus, not deliberate 'bad behaviour', defiance or manipulation. We find that we understand them more just as they understand us more.

I believe we have a responsibility to share important social information with those with autism and we can do so using the evidence-based, effective strategy of Social Stories™. Writing a

Social Story™ takes time and effort – the author must do a lot of work before he even begins to craft the Story. He must abandon his own perspective of a situation, removing his own, and others' opinion or judgement of the event or the child's response and work hard to try to understand the situation from the child's perspective. The child's perspective will lead the author to the missing information and once this has been identified it can then be shared in a Social Story™.

A Social Story™ patiently describes the relevant clues in life, building and clarifying the context of a situation, sharing other people's thoughts, feelings and experiences, and linking these to their reactions and expectations. It does so in a language that is always positive and literally accurate and therefore easily accessible for and respectful of the child with autism. The result should be a uniquely meaningful, patient, non-judgemental, respectful and reassuring description of life.

Carol Gray initiated the Social Story™ approach in 1991 and has defined ten criteria to guide safe and effective Social Story™ writing. These criteria define what a Social Story™ is and the process that researches, writes and illustrates it. Social Stories'™ ten guidelines have been updated by Carol Gray since they were first introduced. The most recent update, Social Stories™ 10.2, which incorporates recent research on context, was published in 2015. There are many trainings and Stories available on the market now that deviate from or ignore the criteria altogether, so it is recommended that if anyone wants to learn how to write a Social Story™ they do so from a Carol Gray approved training source to ensure they receive up-to-date training of high integrity and quality.

What does growing up mean?

As Mark grew and developed it became clear that he was at times completely unaware of his own progress and achievement, and that this often hampered his confidence when he tackled a new skill.

I put together an achievement book (called his Happy Book because it made him so happy to read it), cataloguing all his positive experiences and achievements, which varied from eating noodles to learning to skate. Filled with photos, certificates, swimming badges, written acknowledgements from teachers, his wonderful learning support assistant (LSA) Helen and the family, it was an uplifting experience for all of us to look at and remind ourselves how far he had come. Cuddling up on the sofa under a blanket with this book and Mark was cherished time!

Putting the day into perspective was another challenge, as he frequently labelled the whole day as bad as a result of one thing going awry. Colouring in the home visual timetable, green for good and red for tricky, at the end of the day helped to put things visually and concretely back into perspective for him. Later this technique was carried on into the school day timetable with good effect and also shared effectively with other parents and professionals.

Positive self-reflection was difficult for him, in fact he tended to recall only the negative experiences he had had, so there was a need to concretely remind him of all the positive achievements he had experienced in the past, in order to encourage new learning. After all, we all use the self-talk strategy in reflecting on our own past achievements to galvanise our enthusiasm in order to tackle new challenges that might otherwise seem overwhelming, for example thinking, 'Well I have successfully moved house before, so I can do it again'. This self reflection and episodic memory does not seem to function well for those on the spectrum (Bowler, Gardiner and Grice, 2000) and I frequently find that building it in a conscious way is really helpful for our children.

Social Stories™ are so valuable in this respect as they can effectively combine the past, present and future tenses together in one Story (Gray, 2010). This reflection on prior learning can help the child regain confidence whilst learning a new skill that may require time and perseverance.

In order to share with him some perspective on his own life I wrote this Story, which highlighted the facts that he had learned life-altering skills as his body grew and changed from a baby to a toddler to a child.

Later I used the same format in a Story entitled 'How I found favourite foods' to describe how he tried new foods and discovered favourites as a baby and toddler when he moved from milk to juice and from milk to Jaffa Cakes. This reminded him he had done it before, and in fact had discovered new favourite foods this way.

The format was further developed for a descriptive Story sharing information on puberty. This described how a child's body changes into a young man and gets ready for adulthood. Teaching this idea of being on the continuum of a lifespan is so valuable. I was able to widen his understanding of his life's physical progress as well as his learning progress.

I used the format again to give him information on what others' experience and training had been during their lifespan, which helped when sharing information on why we should respect those who are older and (sometimes) wiser as a result of years of training and experience, as in 'What do my teachers know?'

Later on as I needed to tackle Stories on bereavement, this life Story format was used yet again to demonstrate that an elderly relative had been a baby, then a child, then an adult, then a mother, then a middle aged lady and now a very, very old lady. This Story had photographs of her at all the different life stages. The idea of having lived for many, many years supported the concept that now sadly her body was worn out and broken and may not be able to be fixed. Without this groundwork Mark would have struggled much more with the unfairness of her passing.

Using photos to illustrate this Story is ideal; however, for this book I have supplemented them with drawings.

What does
'growing up' mean?

My name is Mark. When I was born I was
a very small baby. Here is a picture of me as a
very small baby.

I grew and grew. I learned how to sit up. Here
is a picture of me sitting up. In this picture I
am 6 months old.

I grew and grew. I became a toddler. I learned how to walk. Here is a picture of me as a toddler. In this picture I am 1 year old and I am walking.

I grew and grew. I became a child. I learned
how to run and how to push my train. Here is
a picture of me as a child running and pushing
my train. In this picture I am 3 years old.

I am still growing and I am still learning how to do new things. As children get older they learn how to do more things. Many children grow taller as they get older. Growing taller and learning new things is called 'growing up'.

Here is a picture of me now. I am 4 years old. I am still growing and learning new things. I am still growing up.

Stories about calm
What is feeling calm?
What does calm down mean?
How to ask for chill out time

These three Social Stories™ are all about feeling calm, and how to calm down. This series were a set of Stories with one following on from the other. They came about because family members and others would tell Mark to 'calm down' when he became upset and tearful. This might happen for example when unexpected things happened or he lost a game. Sometimes others said this in a quiet soothing voice, but at times in an authoritarian tone, with a raised voice. I noticed that these two words were rarely effective alone, even when spoken in a quiet voice.

I observed his lack of response and questioned if he understood what the words 'calm down' meant. I wondered if he understood what the emotional state of 'calm' was for him. He never used the words himself and looked puzzled when I asked him what the words meant. Children with autism have difficulty identifying emotional states in others and also, most importantly, in themselves (Attwood, 2008). Not being able to identify 'calm' in himself made it impossible for him to work out how to calm himself down.

Explaining what it felt like to be calm was important information I needed to share with Mark. I also needed to point out to him what strategies he was already seeking out and using himself, with success, to achieve a state of calm and then share with him how these could be adapted for use outside of the home.

Following him around the house it became clear that at certain points of the day he sought out activities in which he appeared relaxed and comfortable and I photographed these. These times included when watching a favourite DVD of penguins (one of his special interests), when lying in a warm bubble bath, when stroking the dog (who also looked calm and relaxed too), when feeling his hanky or when listening to his favourite music through his headphones. I then simply commented on what he was doing and how safe and comfy he looked, saying, 'Mark, I am guessing you feel calm'. I did not photograph the times he was happy, animated and excited, for example while playing a video game, because in these situations he was not in a calm, relaxed state.

Initially I put all the photos in a 'calm' book and we would look at them together when he was in a relaxed frame of mind. He looked forward to this and it was clear that just looking at pictures of situations of himself involved in calming activities had a positive calming effect on his mood. I felt his awareness of 'calm' developing.

This picture book later laid the foundation for the illustrations for the first Social Story™ in the calm series 'What is feeling calm?'. Mark engaged with this and was happy to read it, often seeking it out himself. For the purpose of this book I have replaced the photos with pictures in the style and format that was meaningful for Mark.

First I needed to share with him knowledge he was missing – that we all feel anxious or worried at times and we all feel calm sometimes. We all have our own individual methods of calming ourselves down too. A cup of tea, several deep breaths, a walk in the corridor or just popping outside for some fresh air – we all have personal effective strategies that we use to self-regulate and keep ourselves feeling comfortable. Then I needed to highlight to him his own successful strategies for calming himself down. This was the content of the first Story in the set.

The second Story 'What does calm down mean?' was written to describe how some of his soothing strategies may be suitable for him to use when away from home. A piece of his hanky, for example, which he liked to feel between his fingers, could be safely taken out and about sewn inside his shorts or trouser pocket. Permanently fixing it there prevented it being lost or laughed at by peers. Music through headphones at home could be used out and about using smaller portable earphones.

Watching a favourite penguin DVD at home could be converted to counting to ten penguins in his mind, or sequentially naming the different kinds of penguin in height order. Counting alone was not sufficiently calming, but counting penguins was something completely different and a step into his special interest – a really comfy place to be! Another special interest in the Japanese video game 'Mega Man X' allowed Mark to identify with the most diplomatic and pacifist character called X, and call to mind how he would tackle an unexpected situation.

To support the Story I asked family members to state when they were feeling worried/anxious and how they were going to calm themselves down. I role-played my 'cup of tea' strategy with emphasis so it was clear that I too employed a calming strategy.

The third Story in this set of Stories 'How to ask for chill out time' was written because sometimes I observed that he appeared relieved when I told him it was time to go to his room to chill out. This would happen after a behaviour that expressed increasing frustration or upset. So the Story was developed to give Mark an escape phrase, 'I need to chill out', which would allow him to access restorative isolation in the sanctuary of his own bedroom when feeling overwhelmed, without having to stimulate anyone else to put it in place for him.

Once his calming strategies were established and successful for him they helped in lots of other situations, for example turn taking, waiting patiently and when unexpected things happened. I was able also to make reference to them in other Social Stories™ using the coaching sentence 'I will try to stay calm', which now had extra meaning as he had a sensory tool (his hanky), a cognitive tool (thinking about ten penguins) and an escape tool (asking for chill out time), within his reach at all times. He was beginning to build his own portable and immediately accessible self-regulation toolbox (Attwood, 2008).

Several parents have shared with me that making a similar 'calm book' for their child has helped provide some cherished moments looking at it together. The Stories have frequently been requested for other children and have been used successfully after being appropriately individualised for them. I am always careful, however, to make sure anyone considering using this Story as a template for a child has read the following caution.

An important word of caution!

In writing Social Stories™ the author may use only the first or third person or a combination of both (Gray, 2010). When using the first person when describing a child's emotional state the author must be very, very careful that the feeling he describes as the child's own feeling is accurate from the perspective of the child, and not make assumptions from his own neurotypical perspective.

For example, 'I feel calm when my hands and legs are still', may represent how the author wishes the child would feel, or reflect how the author experiences calm. However, this is a concept from their own neurotypical perspective perhaps because when neurotypicals are calm, our bodies and limbs are usually still. Adults, particularly those charged with the care of children, may feel good when our child's hands and feet are still, but it may be that moving the limbs satisfies a sensory need in the child that we do not share or understand. Staying still, without being given another sensory input, may actually be disturbing and uncomfortable for the child with autism and contribute to a feeling of anxiety or panic – the exact opposite emotional state!

This Story worked for Mark because I described strategies he had already sought out and implemented and which were successfully calming him down. I was observing and commenting on these, not suggesting my own ideas. It is interesting to note that all his calming activities had a repetitive element to them. Adaptation of these strategies to be portable does require some creative input, but the actual strategy must remain the same, as it is the child's choice of strategy.

I am so pleased that I chose calm as the first emotion to explore with Mark, before happy or angry emotions, because this work provided a safe foundation to return all emotions to, and engaged Mark with emotion work in a really positive way. I would recommend that this is the first emotion that children with autism work on, as without a good understanding of what calm feels like for them, and what works to calm them down, they have little chance of returning to it in stressful situations.

On a final note, many parents have found the exploration of calm with their child has highlighted their own need for calming strategies for themselves. Keeping calm when your child is in a meltdown is a difficult but important skill to develop, and thinking about what current strategies you use and which can be adapted to be portable can help you too!

What is feeling calm?

Feeling calm is a good feeling. Feeling calm is a comfy safe feeling. Many people like to feel calm. I usually feel calm when I watch my favourite DVD.

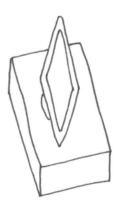

Sometimes I feel calm when I stroke my dog's fur.

Other times I feel calm when I listen to my music with my headphones.

Usually I feel calm when I feel my hanky.

Feeling calm is a good feeling. Other people like being around me when I am feeling calm. At home I may help myself feel calm by:

Feeling my hanky or

Stroking the dog or

Listening to my music in my room or

Watching my favourite DVD or maybe doing something else.

Mum and Dad feel pleased when I feel calm.

What does calm down mean?

Sometimes children feel calm. Sometimes children feel worried. Many children and adults feel worried some of the time and calm some of the time. This is okay.

Usually when someone is worried they try to make themselves feel calmer. This is called 'calming down'. People try to 'calm down' because feeling calm is a good comfy feeling. People usually have a favourite way of calming down.

Mum has a cup of tea when she needs to calm down. This helps her think clearly and make good choices when unexpected things happen.

I am learning how to calm down. Learning how to calm down may help me think clearly and make good choices when unexpected things happen.

Four things that may help me calm down are:

1. Counting to ten penguins

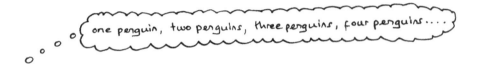

one penguin, two penguins, three penguins, four penguins....

2. Thinking what Mega Man X (my hero) would do in this situation

3. Feeling my hanky in my pocket

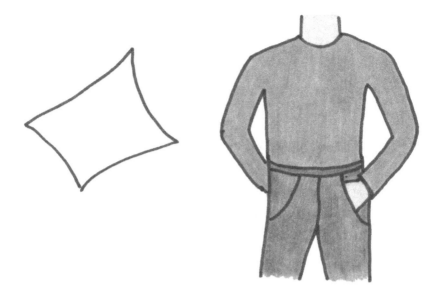

4. Asking for chill out time.

I will work on calming down when unexpected things happen. Mum will be pleased with me.

How to ask for chill out time

Sometimes I feel happy to be with other people.

Other times I want to be in a quiet place alone. This is okay. Everyone feels like this sometimes.

A good place to have quiet time at home is in my room. Mum, Dad and I call having quiet time in my room 'chill out time'.

Mum, Dad and my brothers know that it is important for me to have quiet time on my own sometimes. When I want quiet time alone at home I may say, 'I need to chill out' and go to my room.

When I feel better I can come back.

Saying 'I need to chill out' lets other people know how I am feeling.

I will try to remember to say, 'I need to chill out' when I need to be alone. Mum and Dad and my brothers understand and will be pleased with me.

I am learning to listen

It was clear to me from a very early age that any 'behaviour' Mark displayed was usually a response to a challenge he was experiencing. If I took time to look closely enough, abandoning my own perspective, I could understand the reason behind the response. This allowed me to make adaptations to help him feel more comfortable and also to explore with him how to make these situations more comfortable for himself.

Mark, like many other children with autism, frequently avoids looking at the area of the face around the eyes. High functioning people with autism have described this sensation as uncomfortable or even unbearable. They frequently explain that in order to listen rather than looking at the speaker they need to look at a plain or unstimulating surface, like the floor or a wall. So, for some, discomfort may be the reason they avoid eye contact. For others it may be that looking at someone's face is pointless because they do not receive useful social information from doing so, or perhaps they do not know that they are expected to do so.

However, neurotypical people expect eye contact immediately to know that a child or young person is listening. Looking at the speaker to show attention is an important skill both in school and in the workplace. Without this skill the child may appear to be uninterested and switched off in a world of his own, when in fact he is actively trying to pay full attention.

I have noticed some teaching staff mentioning how a child with autism is staring out of the window or at the floor and needs to learn the skills of paying attention and listening. They are repeatedly asking the child to look at them to show he is listening without understanding that the act of forced looking at a person may render the child incapable of listening at all. To make matters worse the most common time a child is requested to look at an adult's face may be when he has done something perceived as wrong and needing correction. Frequently this is accompanied therefore with a raised voice and a stern facial expression. The result may be overwhelming for the child.

Once Mark was able to tell me he found eye contact 'uncomfy', this Story was written to validate the sensation he was feeling, acknowledge the difficulty this posed him and find a compromise that was respectful of this, but also sharing information on what others need to know.

The Story started with Mum as the speaker, as my face was the most familiar and comfy face he knew, so was a good starting point. Over time 'Mum' in the Story was replaced by 'Dad' and then 'my teacher'. This used the original Story as a master copy, a Story Master, from which others in a similar format could be made to aid generalisation, as described by Carol Gray in her most recent training Social Stories™ 10.2.

Many years later, while working on interview skills in the hunt for a job, we used the Story again as a Story Master, replacing 'Mum' this time with 'the interviewer' and including detail about what the interviewer knew about Mark and the job he was being interviewed for. Thankfully this too was successful!

I am learning to listen

Listening is an important skill to learn. I am learning how to listen to Mum. Mum knows lots of things to tell me. Mum knows how to keep me safe. Mum knows good stories too!

Mum knows I am listening when I am looking at her. Sometimes I may find it uncomfy to look at Mum's face. Mum understands that this may be uncomfy for me. Mum and I have made a plan to keep me comfy. This is okay.

I may look at her for just a short time (count to three penguins) and then look away. In a little while I may look at her again.

Looking for a short time and then looking away from someone's face is called 'glancing'.

When Mum talks to me I will try to glance at her face. Then Mum will know I am listening and I may feel comfy. Mum will be pleased with me.

I am learning to wait patiently

All young children are impatient for quick responses from parents. Learning to wait patiently for a response is always a challenge. Waiting patiently is much more challenging for a child with autism, who may be unaware of other people's thoughts and needs and their occasional priority over their own.

As Mark had been a long time learning to speak, when he did vocalise we responded promptly with delight to encourage more language. He grew used to an instant response. Naturally this became his expectation and he grew frustrated when asked to wait. Understanding his perspective allowed me to guess that he was unaware of his brothers' needs or the fact that as his Mum I could only help one boy at a time. He also needed help with formulating a 'plan B' when his original 'plan A' of instant response was thwarted.

Writing this Story I wanted to share with him information about others' needs and capabilities and also give him gentle guidance on how he might remain calm while waiting. Remaining calm while waiting is of course what 'waiting patiently' is. We had already written a Social Story™ about staying calm and had introduced the tools he was already using to keep himself feeling comfy so I was able to refer to three suggestions in this Story. I included an instant response from me, 'Mark, wait patiently, I will be with you soon', so he always quickly knew that I was aware he was waiting.

This also allowed his siblings to witness that their needs sometimes were higher priority than his.

This Story was a 'slow burner' in that it did not have an instant effect but gradually over time built understanding. It established the concept of 'waiting patiently'. Many of his Stories linked together building concepts on the foundation of another in this way, and I would remind him of and refresh the Calm Story before reading this Story for the first time.

We gently and gradually expanded the concept from waiting patiently for 'Mum' to 'Dad', 'my teacher' and eventually 'an adult'. These followed the same format substituting 'Mum' with the alternative word.

I am learning to wait patiently

Sometimes my Mum talks to me. Other times my Mum helps me. Sometimes my Mum talks to or helps one of my brothers or someone else.

Mum can only help one person at a time. When she is finished Mum will usually be ready to help me. Staying calm while waiting is called waiting patiently.

Mum will help me when she is ready. Mum usually knows when I am waiting. Sometimes Mum says 'Mark, wait patiently, I will be with you soon'.

Waiting patiently is an important grown up skill to learn. I am learning to wait patiently.

Here are three things I may try to help me wait patiently.

1. I may write down or draw what I want to ask her

2. I may feel my hanky in my pocket

3. I may count penguins.

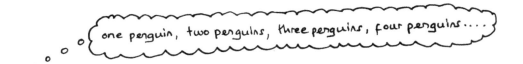

Mum will be pleased with me for waiting patiently. Soon Mum will be able to help me again.

What are kind words?

When Mark entered mainstream education from specialist autism provision he had relatively little language and, although apparently keen to join in and have social interaction (on his terms) with his mainstream classmates, he was unable to initiate this verbally. He enjoyed being chased and learned that if he made a face and said 'na ni ki na na' other children would reliably chase him. However, as he progressed though the early years at school it was clear he was going to need a more friendly method of engaging other children in play.

Picking up on the quick response that insulting words such as 'loser' provoked, despite having little concept of their meaning, he started to use this at home in order to get his brothers to chase him. The response to insulting words is frequently more predictable and although negative it may be comforting in its predictability – it is an interaction of sorts after all.

Because of his theory of mind difficulties Mark was unable to make a good guess about how his brothers might be feeling when he used these words, and unable also to guess which words they would prefer to hear. I needed to share some important information he was missing. I felt a Social Story™ on which type of words other children find friendly would be helpful.

A Social Story™ avoids negative words in the vocabulary to give a positive and reassuring tone so I avoided words like 'rude' or 'bad' (Gray, 2010). After all, up until this point telling him 'not to use bad words' had not worked, partly because this gave no indication of which words might be more effective to use, and partly because this just described what he was doing at present, which was not helpful. The use of the negative word 'not' here was also difficult for him to understand. I decided that 'kind' and its negated counterpart 'unkind' were the categories of words I was most comfortable in teaching him. 'Friendly' and 'unfriendly' would have been an alternative choice.

A Social Story™ should only include vocabulary that the child understands, so first I needed to develop his understanding of the words I wanted to use in the Story. I spent a long, long time watching Mark at play with his brothers. Each time he said any positive word or phrase I would comment on it positively and animatedly saying 'Oh that's a kind word – well done! I am going to write that down on the blue paper!' and I would write it on a piece of blue paper in dark blue pen under the title 'Kind Words'. Mark's favourite colour is blue. This piece of paper I put up on the notice board in the kitchen.

Whenever a negative word or phrase was used, I would comment on it quietly stating 'Oh that is an unkind word; that goes on the red paper'. Mark does not like the colour red. The words would be written in dark red pen under the title 'Unkind Words'. The red paper was then placed in the drawer out of sight.

I encouraged his brothers to ignore, as much as possible, any negative words he used and instead respond quickly to positive words with great enthusiasm. His brothers were keen to help!

From time to time I would point out the blue paper and comment on the kind words I had heard Mark use. In this way I was trying to gradually reverse the positive reinforcement of a predictable response to negative or unkind words and at the same time develop Mark's understanding about what 'kind' and 'unkind' words were.

The Social Story™ was then written to explain how others like kind words. This gave Mark information on what words other children would like him to use, information that he was unable to pick up for himself. Within the Story I put a reminder of where he could find a list of kind words and phrases he might choose – pinned up on the kitchen notice board.

This Story was another 'slow burner' – it took time to be effective – but there were clear early signs of effort to choose kind words around others and when these proved more effective than unkind words the choice of vocabulary definitely changed. A praise Story for his effort quickly followed!

People who know Mark now would definitely describe his vocabulary as kind and friendly. Occasionally video games or YouTube clips will influence his choice, and he may struggle in identifying which language is suitable for which context, so there continues to be a need for ongoing discussion from time to time about how different words may make others feel, but this is now done on a foundation built by the successful work around, and the implementation of the following short Story.

On a final note I have noticed that the word 'kind' is frequently used when directing the behaviour and play of children with autism, and I would recommend that understanding of its meaning is always explored first.

What are kind words?

Many children and grown ups use words to talk to each other. Sometimes children and grown ups use words to ask questions too.

Some words are kind words. Some words are unkind words. Kind words usually make people feel good. Using kind words is a friendly thing to do. Many children like to play with children who use kind words.

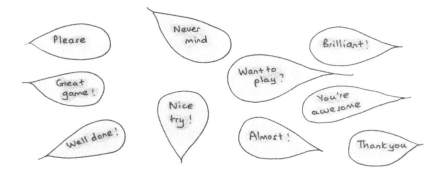

Some kind words are written on the blue paper in the kitchen at home. I will try to use kind words when I talk to children and grown ups.

What is taking turns?
I am learning to share toys

Learning about sharing or taking turns is a challenge for children with autism and Mark certainly found it very difficult. The most public and obvious example of this would occur at the playground near the slide that he loved. Taking his perspective it is easy to understand why. Theory of mind allows neurotypicals to accurately, continually and subconsciously consider other people's feelings or needs. Automatically having other people's wishes or needs in mind allows us to understand sharing, taking turns and queuing. Instantly we understand that other children want to go down the slide too. Without this understanding waiting for a turn in a line or queue makes little sense. I like the slide, there is the slide, off I go!

So for Mark, like many other children with autism, there was a need to share this critical missing information with him if he was to effectively understand and cooperate with turn taking at the playground or anywhere else.

Cherie Meiner (2003) describes in her children's book *Share and Take Turns* how we wait for a turn when we cannot use something at the same time and this seemed a beautifully simple explanation of why we take turns and queue. I have used this concept in the following Story.

There are many situations at school and at home where the family or class has to share a resource because only one person can use it at a time, for example class computer, playground equipment like a slide, collecting our dinner from the dinner hatch, Mum's attention, the teacher's attention, queuing at a checkout – the list is endless. Most of these situations cause difficulty for a child with autism.

Adults too have to take turns when only one person can use something at a time, so examples of these situations were helpful to point out. At the time of writing this Story the football World Cup was on, which provided great visual examples of turn taking at penalties. I also spent a lot of time around implementation of this Story pointing out to Mark other real-life situations where this applied and noting how people queued to take a turn.

Unfortunately, because human behaviour is not always compliant with the rules we teach our children, further Stories were required, 'What does jumping the queue mean?' and 'What to think and do when someone jumps the queue'.

Learning to share a toy was also a major challenge. For those special items that Mark carried everywhere with him, like his Brum car or Postman Pat van, sharing was never going to be successful. These items were much more than play items, they were familiar props that allowed him to navigate a chaotic world and the distress their absence caused was clear evidence of this. To learn to share he had to begin with toys that were not so valuable to him. So the Story allowed him to refuse to share a special toy and find another toy to share instead. It also showed that usually when playtime was finished the toys returned to their owners, which relieved his anxiety around the 'loss' of the toy.

As Mark grew older, further Stories were written about resolving the conflict that arises when another child does not return a toy after a swap, or refuses to share or simply takes his toy.

The 'I am learning to share toys' Story was just a beginning.

What is taking turns?

Many playgrounds have a slide. Usually I want to go down the slide.

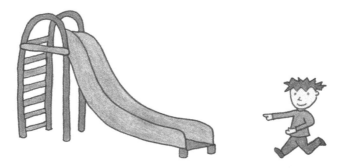

Sometimes other children in the playground want to go down the slide too.

There is room for only one child to go down the slide safely at a time. Children usually take turns to go down the slide. Taking turns is a fair way of sharing one thing that everyone cannot use at the same time.

To take turns the children line up at the steps of the slide. This is called 'forming a queue or line'. The first child to wait by the slide is at the front of the queue and has the first turn down the slide. This is fair because they were the first to get to the slide. The second child in the queue has the second turn and the third child has the third turn, and so on.

Sometimes I will be at the front of the queue, sometimes I will be somewhere in the middle of the queue and sometimes I will be at the end of the queue. My place in the queue depends on when I joined the queue. This is okay. As each child in front of me has his or her turn I am getting closer to my turn. This is how queues work.

Children in the queue usually try to wait patiently until it is their turn. Once a child has gone down the slide he or she may join the end of the queue to wait for another turn.

Taking turns is a fair way of everyone having a go down the slide. Children usually like to play with children who take turns.

Grown ups often take turns too. Grown ups take turns at the petrol station filling the car with petrol.

Children and grown ups take turns to pay at the checkout in the supermarket.

Children footballers and grown up footballers take turns with shooting penalties!

Learning to take turns is a clever grown up thing to do. I am learning to take turns.

I am learning to share toys

Sometimes it is fun to play with my toys on my own. Sometimes I want to play with another child's toys. Sometimes another child wants to play with my toys.

One way to play with another child's toy is to share them. One way of sharing is playing together with the toys.

Another way of sharing is swapping toys. Swapping toys means the other child may play with my toy while I play with their toy.

At the end of the playing time children usually give back the toys to their owners. Sharing a toy with another child is being friendly.

Sometimes I have a toy that is extra special to me, like Brum. I may not want to share it with another child. This is okay.

I may choose another toy to share.

When I share I am being kind and friendly. Other children usually like to play with kind and friendly children. I am learning about sharing toys.

What is a conversation?

Learning to take turns in listening and talking requires understanding of the context of the conversation, being mindful of another's thoughts and feelings, reading facial expressions, interpreting intonation and gestures and making social sense of them, and then responding in a way that is sensitive to the feelings of that person. All of these skills, which happen automatically for neurotypicals without conscious thought, need to be learned and consciously thought through for the child with autism.

Once his language was established Mark enjoyed talking, particularly about his special interest. However, he tended to be uninterested in what other people were saying unless it was also on that topic. To teach the art of taking turns in listening and talking I therefore started with his first choice topic, his special interest, so that he would be comfortable learning about the particularly difficult challenge of listening to another person within a conversation. I used a conversation between Mark and myself as a starting point so that the topic and the person he was talking with were the most familiar and comfortable they could be. I had to research and learn about his special interest in order to talk about it in an interesting way for him to engage. As Mark has developed different interests throughout his life I have always tried hard to learn about each as best I can so that we continue to communicate well. Each time I explore a new fascination he has I learn a little more about Mark himself!

Exploration of his own perspective through Carol Gray's Comic Strip Conversation technique (Gray, 1994) helped me to understand what information he was missing and allowed him to see other people's thoughts and speech in a concrete and permanent way so he could study them for as long as he needed.

This Story was written to explain what a conversation was and why it was only fair to listen and let the other person have their turn speaking. I explored through Comic Strip Conversation how when two people speak at the same time without taking turns to listen, their words 'bump' into each other and become muddled up and difficult to understand. Spoken words are transient and invisible so making this concrete and visible using Carol Gray's technique (Gray, 1994) was invaluable. The illustration here came from our drawing conversation.

He had learned about turn taking prior to starting this Story, having read the turn taking Story and also with very hands on practical games with another child involving sand play, water play and play with cars over a long period of time.

Mark has his best conversations, on topic and reciprocal, when he is talking to someone he trusts, who also enjoys the topic he loves. It is wonderful to witness, and I am always delighted to note how when he is comfy enough he uses much improved eye contact, facial expressions and gestures. This then is the answer to friendship for him, and possibly for other children with autism – to find those who share the same interests!

We are always working together on improving conversation with people he does not know well, and expanding the range of topics he is comfortable to talk about. This will always be a work in progress but it is a continual joy to see the success of Social Stories™ in this area so far.

Later Stories were written on how to stay on someone else's topic, change topic or ask questions on their topic. These skills follow on from understanding turn taking within a conversation, and waiting for a gap to interrupt a conversation.

What is a conversation?

Mum likes to talk to me and to listen to me. Sometimes Mum needs to talk to someone else. This is okay. When Mum is finished talking and listening to the other person she will usually talk to me again.

When two people talk at the same time it is difficult to listen and understand because the words 'bump' into each other and muddle up. This is why people usually take turns in listening and talking.

Taking turns in listening and talking is called having a conversation. A conversation may have two or more people taking part. People like having conversations with people who take turns to talk and listen.

Sometimes it is easy to listen to another person talk. This usually happens when they are talking about something interesting to me.

Other times it is more difficult to listen to another person talk. This usually happens when they are talking about something uninteresting to me.

Still, it is important to listen because the person is having their turn and that is fair. Sometimes I may learn something interesting. Soon it will be my turn to speak again.

How to interrupt a conversation

Interrupting a conversation politely is a skill that many neurotypical adults fail to achieve. Having spent a long time encouraging Mark to speak by responding immediately to any vocalisation, he was very used to eliciting an instant response. If not responded to immediately, he would try to pull me away from the conversation. Learning to wait patiently needed therefore to be established first, with some portable and immediately accessible strategies for him to employ whilst waiting. This took some time. Once that was understood it was easier to ask him to wait patiently for a gap in the conversation. To begin with I acted these out with large obvious gaps and responded immediately to his 'Excuse me'. Over time I allowed the gaps to become less obvious and more difficult for him to recognise. The Social Story™ then encouraged him to tap me on the arm with an 'excuse me' phrase. Identifying a specific, non-personal place to touch on another person would be difficult for the child with autism so it is clearly defined within the Story. Following a tap on the arm I would wait a few seconds and continue the conversation, then give him my full attention when a gap came along. Little by little I was able to extend the wait until he was okay with waiting a reasonable length of time.

'Mum' was replaced by 'Dad', and then the names of his brothers, family members and friends in order to generalise the principle of interruption of a conversation. Of course it was important too that the Story included the exception to the rule that in times of danger he interrupted straight away!

Learning not to interrupt when someone was involved in a telephone conversation with an unseen person was also difficult to navigate. Teaching about telephone calls started early with two play telephones in the same room, where he could clearly see the other person. I then separated them gradually into two rooms through an open door so he could still see the person. The real telephone was trickier as there were no visual clues as to whom I was speaking. Using photos of regular callers kept close to the phone I was able to place their photo close to the handset and point to their face. I put the phone on speakerphone to allow him to hear their voice. Mark has a good audio memory so this was really helpful. Over time the loudness of the voice was faded and eventually speakerphone switched off with just the photo remaining. Nowadays automatic caller recognition can show photos on the handset or mobile, and visual displays on tablets during calls must make this process so much easier!

Every time Mark tried to comply with the gentle coaching within a Story he was praised enthusiastically. A Social Story™ was quickly written to praise him for his effort and shared with members of the family. Carol Gray emphasises that 50 per cent of all Stories written for a child should recognise the effort and achievements of the child (Gray, 2010). This motivates the child to keep trying even when not immediately successful, building self-esteem as noted by Howley and Arnold (2005).

How to interrupt a conversation

Sometimes when Mum is talking to someone I want to ask her a question or tell her something. Stopping the conversation so that I can say something is called 'interrupting' a conversation.

Learning how to interrupt a conversation with good manners is an important skill to learn. I may wait for a gap in the conversation and then say, 'Excuse me'. This lets Mum know I have something to say.

Sometimes it is tricky to work out when there is a gap. When it is tricky I may tap Mum gently on the arm and say, 'Excuse me'. Mum likes me to tap her gently on the arm because it lets Mum know I have something to say. When the next gap comes, Mum will usually try to give me her attention.

While I am waiting for a gap or for Mum to finish her conversation I may need to work on waiting patiently. Mum is pleased when I wait patiently.

Sometimes I want to tell Mum about a danger. When this happens it is okay to interrupt a conversation without waiting for a gap.

I am learning how to interrupt a conversation.

What are good manners?

Good manners are important for any child. But for a child with autism who may make many social mistakes they are critical. On many occasions Mark's good manners have allowed others to recognise his unusual response as a lack of understanding rather than a cheeky or rude response. An example of this was when asked by a teacher at school 'Would you like to get your Maths book out please Mark?' he replied, very literally and honestly, 'No, thank you'. The 'thank you' here allowed the teacher to think about his response and arrive at the correct conclusion that he was not being defiant but interpreting her question very literally!

So the simplest manners are probably the most important – those of saying 'please' and 'thank you'. Our children will require others to help them from time to time throughout their life and having this established early on will make life just a little bit easier for them.

I initially wrote very simple Social Stories™ about please and thank you. Mark needed to know how these words made others feel. We modelled it with exaggerated 'please' and 'thank you' to each other extensively within the home, stating how it made us feel.

Later on when people commented on what 'good manners' Mark had, I noted his puzzled expression and that he did not say 'thank you'. When we talked it became clear that although he was learning good manners, he had no idea what the words 'good manners' meant. I wrote the following Story to explain the meaning and it was successful for him and also other children.

What are good manners?

Sometimes I need help to do something. This is okay. Everyone needs help sometimes. When I need help it is okay to ask an adult or another child to help me.

Saying 'please' when asking for help shows the person I will be pleased if they can help me.

Saying 'thank you' when someone has helped me shows that I have noticed that they have helped me. I am usually pleased that they have helped me.

Saying please and thank you is called having good manners. Many people think having good manners is smart and kind. Other people usually like being around people with good manners.

Many people have good manners. Sometimes people forget. This is okay, they may remember another time. I will try to have good manners and remember to say 'please' and 'thank you'.

What are table manners?

In our first flat we were unable to fit a dining table in the kitchen or elsewhere so we would eat sitting up at a countertop side by side. Eating side by side is efficient and quick but it reduces any opportunities for children to see what others are eating, doing or saying, and therefore is not a shared time together. Sitting side by side in front of a favourite television programme or DVD is a good way to keep a child entertained and eating, and I admit that I have done this in the past in order to help Mark eat a sufficient amount of food, but it was not helping his social eating skills.

So much of our sociable behaviour centres around sharing food: in the school, college or workplace canteen, at a dinner out, visiting a restaurant with friends or relatives, eating together at a party or at a family celebration like a christening or wedding. Not being comfortable with social eating may be a significant disadvantage in being sociable, so when we had moved to a home with more space, the first thing we did was to buy a fold-down dining table so Mark and his brothers could sit around a table with us to eat together.

I believe that this social gathering to eat from a very young age is critical to the development of early social skills and lays a very important foundation for cooperation around a nursery school table with a group of other children. Sharing dishes, the tomato sauce and the jug of juice also leads to a more concrete understanding of sharing common school or workplace items.

But this is undoubtedly a difficult area for children with autism. To ease into sitting together I always put Mark's seat a little further away from his neighbour and only called him to the table when absolutely everything was ready to reduce his waiting time. This waiting time was gradually increased in tiny increments over a long period. To prevent a problem with repeated calling to come for lunch and dinner I rang a dinner bell, which was later replaced by a wireless doorbell. This meant that he was less likely to have been provoked by words or shouts to hurry down. A simple Social Story™ describing the purpose of the bell and that he had five minutes closure time before coming down helped establish this support.

Because being social at a table with others is sufficiently challenging in itself I always used to work on introducing a new food at a different part of the day when he could tackle it with me alone to reduce additional social stress.

The two table rules I tried to establish first were waiting until everyone was served before starting, and also waiting until everyone had finished before leaving the table. This is a big challenge for someone who does not enjoy the social part of the meal, and Mark would be the first to admit that he still needs prompting from time to time. Sharing a meal with family and friends is, however, now frequently a pleasure for Mark if due consideration is given to his needs.

When we ate out as a family at an unfamiliar restaurant we rang ahead and tried to ensure the menu included something he liked. We always brought Mark to the table as close to the meal as possible to reduce the time he had to wait before the food was served. I would bring a tiny jam pot filled with peanut butter and one of ketchup as transfer foods so that he could always enjoy bread or chips and would not go hungry. Being hungry while tackling a stressful social experience is not the best combination! I also would bring a Game Boy® or small handheld activity he could distract himself with if there was a long delay.

Where he sat at a table when we were out was also important and we would choose his place where there was a wall behind him so people would not be moving behind him randomly. We would also try to choose a table in the least busy and noisy section of the restaurant away from any music speakers or doors. As the years have passed I have become quite deaf myself, and I find myself making the same choice for my comfort too. I certainly have a better understanding now of the challenge of a noisy place for someone whose sensory input is impaired or different.

Designing verbal games that required his attention, on subjects he was interested in, really helped keep him at the table. Some examples are naming characters from his favourite television series such as 'Sharpe' or types of car from 'Top Gear'. He is always much better than all of us at these games! This has been a starting point to engage him in conversation during and at the end of the meal. In order to help him to develop a sense of perspective on the day we would also try and each have a turn saying what had been good about our day and what had been not so good. This also allowed him to hear other people's experience, information that he would not have had otherwise.

We are now able to go to restaurants and are confident he will manage to sit at the table comfortably for the duration of the meal, provided some allowances are made, and get pleasure from doing so.

What are table manners?

Table manners are rules for eating at a table that keep others comfy. Following these rules is a friendly and respectful thing to do. Sometimes when children and adults follow these rules others say they have good table manners.

Table manners are unwritten rules. Many children learn them from their parents. Other people usually like eating with people who have good table manners.

Eating lunch and dinner together is a time children and adults share. Waiting until everyone is served before starting to eat means everyone starts their meal at about the same time together and no one gets left behind. A person who has good table manners usually waits until everyone is served before starting to eat their meal.

When a meal is finished it is good manners to wait until others are finished too before leaving the table. This way no one gets left behind.

There are many table manners to learn. Mum and Dad will teach me more as I get older. I am learning to have good table manners.

What does 'excuse me' mean?

I first taught Mark that 'excuse me' was a phrase we used when we had made an unexpected body noise. This was a simple Social Story™ that worked well for most situations, however after one particular experience I became aware that Mark now needed help in identifying the different contexts that influenced the many other meanings of 'excuse me'.

We had finished a swimming lesson and were walking past the entrance to a theatre that was inside the leisure complex. A crowd of people was gathered there, waiting to go inside. An elderly man was moving slowly through the crowd trying to get to the coffee shop on the other side of the crowd. As he moved he called out 'excuse me' repeatedly. Now Mark's understanding, as he had been taught, was that the man must have been making loads of 'body noises', so his response was to laugh. People in the crowd were a little shocked at his response. I obviously needed to widen his understanding of the different meanings of 'excuse me' in different contexts.

Peter Vermeulen's recent hypothesis of autism as a context blindness (Vermeulen, 2012) has led to an improved understanding of the need to highlight contexts in real-life situations for people with autism. It is important to explain the different meanings of words and phrases in different contexts, providing the child or adult has the cognitive ability to understand. Social Stories™ are the perfect medium to do this and, I believe, this is one of the reasons they have been so effective in helping my son and others over many years. We returned home and later that day explored the different meanings of 'excuse me' with a drawing conversation. The following Story evolved from that drawing conversation.

This was the first Story that encouraged looking for clues around a situation and although this inevitably takes time, because the child or young person with autism needs to consciously analyse the clues, it can be effective and was in this case. Of course the four meanings of excuse me are only the most common situations where excuse me is used. There are other more complex situations to share, but many of these involve more difficult concepts like sarcasm that are trickier to figure out in the heat of the moment. In time these were addressed too, also with Social Stories™, in the form of Social Articles.

The first time this Story was written it had photographs and much less text. At the time Mark was interested in the cartoon 'Inspector Gadget' and liked the idea of looking for clues; however, he needed guidance on what clues to look for. The photo of him in a detective-like coat and hat acted as a reminder of 'looking for clues'. It should be noted that Mark did not expect to be wearing his coat and hat in daily life to work out clues, and understood that the picture was a reminder only. The inclusion of this picture, therefore, is an example of how a Story is crafted for the individual, and may not be suitable for other children without adaptation. Several of the pictures relating to interrupting are taken from that previous Story and are a visual reminder of the content of that Story.

Over time, as Mark's understanding of language improved along with his reading I was able to share more information with him in a more complex way, and this is the version included here. This Story is much longer and holds more information than most Stories. It is mainly written in the third person but also uses the first person in the final paragraph. It makes use of longer sentences with commas, and a more advanced vocabulary that matched Mark's exact cognitive level at the time. A Social Story™ or Article should always be pitched at the child's level and neither patronise nor stretch them. I would call this Story a Social Article.

What does 'excuse me' mean?

'Excuse me' usually means 'I am sorry'. 'Excuse me' may mean different things in different situations. Sometimes it is easy to understand which situation is happening. Sometimes it is more difficult. Usually there are clues around the situation that may help.

Learning to look for these clues, like a detective, may help work out which situation is happening.

Here are four meanings of excuse me:

1. Sometimes a person says 'excuse me' when they have made an unexpected noise from their body. Sometimes the noise may be a cough or a sneeze. Sometimes a noise may come up from the person's tummy and out of the mouth. This noise is usually called a 'burp' or 'belch'. Sometimes a noise comes out from the person's bottom. This noise is usually called a 'fart'.

Saying 'excuse me' is a way of saying sorry for making a noise that may be uncomfy for other people to hear or smell. Sometimes a person may cover their mouth with their hand. The clue is usually the noise or smell.

2. Sometimes people say 'excuse me' when moving through a space where others have to move to let them by. Sometimes this happens in a crowd of people waiting for something. Sometimes this happens when there is a small space to move through, like getting to a cinema seat or maybe something else. Saying 'excuse me' in this situation is a way of saying sorry for disturbing people so that the person can move past them.

Usually the clue is someone trying to move past other people through a small space or through a crowd. Usually a person follows it with 'thank you' as people move to let them pass.

3. Sometimes people say 'excuse me' when they cannot hear. Saying 'excuse me' is a way of saying sorry for asking someone to repeat what they have just said.

The clue is that someone is speaking or has spoken and another person is trying to listen. Occasionally a person may turn their head so that their ear is closer to the speaker. Sometimes a person may cup their hand around their ear or raise their hand.

4. Sometimes people say 'excuse me' when they are waiting to speak in a conversation. Saying 'excuse me' is a way of letting the people in the conversation know they have something to say and saying sorry for interrupting the conversation. It is a way of politely interrupting others.

The clue here is that a person is talking in a conversation with one or more than one other person.

Sometimes a person saying 'excuse me' in this situation may gently tap the person speaking on the arm.

These meanings of 'excuse me' are common ones. This means they happen a lot. There are other meanings of 'excuse me' too. Mum will explain these to me as I grow older.

Next time I hear someone say 'excuse me' I will try to look for the clues in the situation. This will help me make a best guess of what 'excuse me' means in a situation. I am learning about the meanings of 'excuse me' and I am learning to look for clues too!

Why do I write thank you letters?

Understanding the social importance of saying thank you requires an understanding of how the other person may feel when thanked. Because of theory of mind difficulties this important information needs to be shared with the young person with autism.

Learning to thank someone for a gift, or for help given that has made a child happy seems logical and sensible, and is relatively easy to teach. However, learning to say thank you for a present that has disappointed, or for help that has not been useful, is more challenging for an honest, literal and logical child with autism. Carol Gray has written many excellent Stories around this topic, available in her book, *The New Social Story*™ *Book* (Gray, 2010) including Stories around what to say and do when a present disappoints.

When it came to writing a thank you letter for a present Mark disliked I needed to clarify further for him just exactly what he was thanking the person for, as to him there seemed to be no logical sense in thanking someone for a disappointment, particularly in writing. As he had recently received a book on boats as a present (which had disappointed him) we explored his understanding of the task of buying a present for someone else with a Comic Strip Conversation (Gray, 1994). Mark had a special interest in the *Titanic* at the time, like many other children with autism. Many people on hearing he liked the *Titanic* would presume he would be interested in boats in general, and the gift they chose subsequently would disappoint him. He could, however, after talking it through in a drawing conversation, concretely see how they were trying to buy something he liked.

I supported this Story with some practical groundwork first, taking Mark to choose another child a present. We tried together to think about what the child might like, reflecting on what the child liked to talk about (this took a long time because it involved also talking about what Mark liked, and visiting the things Mark liked in the shop first). Then we queued to buy the present, the card and some wrapping paper. Instead of wrapping and sending the parcel from the Post Office on my own, which would have been much quicker and much less stressful, I took Mark with me and we queued again. The whole process took a long time!

The next day, when we had recovered, I completed the Social Story™ for him. I included illustrations that came from our experience the day before. This Story, fresh from a recent experience, had an immediate big impact and he was happy to write a very brief thank you letter for his disappointing birthday present that afternoon.

Interestingly over time Mark remembered the phrase 'it was very kind of you' after writing it in lots of thank you letters and subsequently used it spontaneously when someone helped him or gave him something. A great result all round! This Story has been used after adaptation for others with success.

Why do I write thank you letters?

Sometimes people send me a present in the post. My Granny and Grandad sometimes send me a present in the post. Sometimes for my birthday and at Christmas people in my family send me a present in the post.

To send a present in the post usually takes a lot of time. First the person goes to the shops. The person tries hard to choose the kind of present I like. When they find a present they queue at the cashier to pay for it.

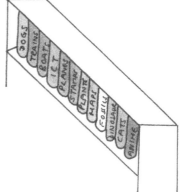

Then the person takes the present home and wraps it in a parcel. Next the person takes the parcel to the Post Office. Usually there is a queue at the Post Office to send a parcel.

Doing all these things takes a lot of time and effort!

Usually people like to know if I have received the parcel safely. Sending a thank you letter is a way of telling the person that I have received the parcel.

Sometimes the present makes me happy, sometimes it disappoints me. This is okay, this happens with presents sometimes. It is easy to choose a present for myself, it is usually more tricky to choose the right present for another person.

Sending a thank you letter shows the person that I am pleased they TRIED to find the right present for me. Sending a thank you letter shows the person I appreciate the effort they have made in going to the shops, choosing me a present, buying it, wrapping it and sending it to me.

Sending a thank you letter usually makes the person feel happy. When writing a thank you letter many people say something like 'it was very kind of you to send me a present'. I will try to remember to write 'thank you' letters when people send me presents.

What is a hand dryer?

The first time my son used a hand dryer he was terrified. Despite my careful instructions his response was of total fear and panic. I should have written a Social Story™ about using a hand dryer before he met one! I decided some serious groundwork needed to be in place before we tried again. I visited the closest public toilet with a hand dryer, on my own, and tried to imagine the experience from his perspective. There were many sensory issues that were clearly going to be uncomfortable for him. The sensations of noise, vibration and pressure of the air coupled with the unpredictable nature of the off/on system made for a perfect storm with his sensory difficulties. To make matters worse there was a queue and social pressure to move quickly through the drying process so others waiting could use it too.

I then had a drawing conversation with Mark. He described his fear that the machine was going to 'get' him. This was not an unreasonable assumption as it made the noise of an engine starting and accelerating towards him! I showed him in photographs that it was fixed to the wall and could not move away from it by itself. This was information that he was clearly reassured by, so I noted it to include in my Social Story™.

To tackle the difficulty around the sensory issues we worked initially with the hair dryer, which he was now comfortable with. This too had taken time to establish – using the dryer on a low setting and holding it far away, moving it closer and closer gradually over time. The sensation of warm air blown onto skin is different to warm air being blown onto the scalp and hair so this needed to be introduced slowly again. So we used the hair dryer on our hands at a low setting far away, moving it closer gradually and then moving it on to higher settings over time. We watched our wet hands dry together under the stream of warm air, and this built confidence and understanding of the process in a slow controlled way. This culminated in Mark drying my hands, and allowing me to dry his with the hair dryer.

Other children have successfully used this Story with adaptation. One child who found the noise of a hand dryer to be intolerable benefited from a recording of a hand dryer at low volume being played within the Story with the addition of a couple of sentences as follows 'A hand dryer blows out warm air. The hand dryer may sound like this… This is okay.' The volume of the hand dryer recording was gradually increased over time. Work then needed to be done on the different sounds made by different hand dryers.

For another child we made a small picture book and took a photo of every hand dryer he met, placing each photo in the book with 'and this is a photo of a hand dryer' written beneath each photo. The title of the book was 'Photos of hand dryers'. These were used in a Story Master to build generalisation as described by Carol Gray in the most recent training Social Stories™ 10.2.

The illustrations in this Story must be photographs of current hand dryers that the child has had experience with. Hand dryer technology is constantly changing so the photos must be up to date. When I wrote the Story for Mark we used photos from familiar places and toilets he had visited. I have used drawings in their place here to show what kind of illustrations need to be in place.

Over the years I have found that hand dryers are a source of fear and anxiety to many children with autism. So much so that many will refuse to use public facilities and may avoid toilets in school and the workplace as a result.

What is a hand dryer?

I am learning to use the toilet. Usually after I use the toilet I wash my hands and dry them. At home I dry my hands on a towel. The towel at home usually looks like this.

After I use the toilet and wash my hands at other people's houses I dry my hands on a towel. The towel is usually close to the sink. The towel at Granny's house usually looks like this.

Sometimes when I am out I need to use the public toilets.

Sometimes in public toilets there are paper towels for drying hands. This is okay. There is usually a bin for the used towels in a public toilet. When I have finished drying hands the used paper towel goes in the bin.

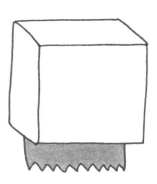

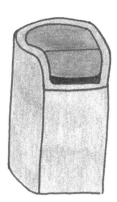

Sometimes in public toilets there is a hand dryer. A hand dryer is a machine for drying wet hands.

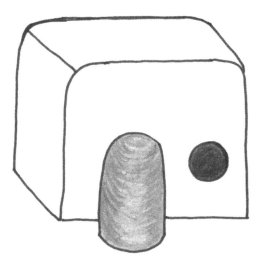

The machine is fixed to the wall and cannot move. Its job is to blow out warm air. The warm air blowing out dries wet hands. This is okay – the machine is doing a good job!

The warm air makes a noise like a hair dryer. The warm air from a hair dryer dries my hair when it is wet. This is okay. This is a picture of the hair dryer at home drying my hair.

The warm air from a hand dryer dries wet hands. Hands need to be close to the warm air coming out of the dryer for the dryer to do its job. Usually there is a picture on the dryer showing the best place to put hands. An adult will show me the best place to put my hands.

Some hand dryers turn on when hands are near the machine. Some machines have a button to press. Some machines turn on when a person is nearby. The machine will usually switch off after a short while.

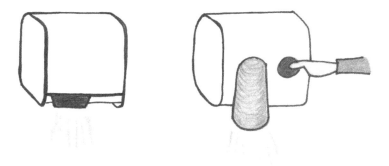

I am learning to dry my hands using a hand dryer or a towel.

Mum will be really pleased with me if I try to use a hand dryer or a towel to dry my hands.

How to find another favourite food

In common with so many children with autism Mark has sensory issues with the taste, smell, texture and look of new foods. It was particularly the difference in these modalities that prevented him from trying new foods. He quickly lost trust in our description of a new food as 'yummy' when it proved to be not only distasteful for him but also uncomfortable. I needed to expand his diet without causing distress and I felt helping him reflect on his past achievements might help him accept trying a new food in the future. I wanted him then to decide for himself what was comfy, after gradually becoming familiar with the new sensations. Social Stories™ allow past, present and future to be linked together (Gray, 2010) to encourage a child facing what seems an insurmountable challenge to reflect on past achievements.

This required a retrospective look at the foodstuffs Mark had already tried and liked, going back as far as babyhood. I was well placed as his Mum to remember! I talked about and drew all Mark's favourite foods with him. He suggested his current ones – peach juice and Jaffa Cakes, and I drew them. We labelled them favourite foods. I suggested milk was his favourite drink when he was a baby. I drew a picture of him drinking his milk as a baby and smiling, and next to it I drew a picture of him drinking juice and smiling. We talked about what would have happened if Mark had never tried juice? He said he would be sad because he liked juice.

I congratulated him on having discovered a favourite drink and told Mark I would write him a Story about his favourite foods. This first Story established the self-refection that he had already tried new foods and drinks and in doing so had discovered new favourites.

The second Story outlined a plan we had agreed on together. It was built on the idea that maybe another favourite would be fun to discover. In the plan Mark was in charge of each step and was not forced. His comfort was of paramount importance. Trying each step for as long as he needed allowed his sensations to very gradually get used to the new experience. The time limit for each step was dictated by when he felt comfortable with going to the next step. If at any step it was too uncomfortable to continue, then he had made an important discovery and we respected that. We began with foods that were close to his favourites in colour, texture and taste. When all the pressure was removed and he was in more control of what was 'comfy' for him he was more able and willing to try a new food. One at a time, very, very gradually, we were able to introduce several new foods.

These two Stories were not only successful for trying new foods but also became a good template for trying new experiences in general. Through this ongoing experience Mark also regained trust in my understanding and respect for his different perspective on life. Many years later, as a teenager, his brother's girlfriend Harriett, whom he trusted implicitly, suggested to him that as he liked spaghetti he might like noodles. She persuaded him to visit a local noodle bar with her where she asked the staff to produce noodles and chicken with no vegetables, pork, seafood or other ingredients. He loved it.

The positive consequences of this ability to discover a new favourite food have been immense. During his college years Mark would visit the same noodle restaurant independently for lunch as take away or eat in every Friday! The wonderfully kind staff greeted him each week, showing him to a quiet table with 'The usual sir?' and I would meet him there for lunch and a chat. College was presenting new challenges on a daily basis. There was a need for a comfortable break in the middle of the day, which would allow him to talk through the morning's events with his 'coach' and prepare for the afternoon! Eating his favourite dish of noodles at the noodle bar was concrete evidence of his ability to navigate new challenges. He would return to college reminded of this, with his self-esteem bucket and stomach refilled!

I would never ever have predicted this outcome from our original struggles. Encouragement I hope for all those who struggle with trying new foods.

How to find another favourite food

My name is Mark. When I was a baby I drank milk from a bottle. Here is a picture of me as a baby, drinking from my bottle.

Milk was my favourite drink. When I was older I tried juice and discovered that juice tasted good. Now juice is another favourite drink.

Then I tried a Jaffa Cake and discovered that Jaffa Cakes taste really good. Now Jaffa Cakes are my most favourite food.

Trying new foods is a good way to discover favourite foods. Many children and adults have more than one favourite food. Having many favourite foods helps keep the body healthy and working well.

I will work on trying another food. I may decide I like it. I may decide I dislike it. This is okay. I may make an important discovery and find another favourite food!

Our plan to discover another favourite food

Sometimes a food feels comfy to eat. Sometimes a food feels uncomfy to eat. Mum and I have made a plan to help me stay comfy when I am trying a new food.

Our plan has four steps. Following the four steps takes time. One step may take longer than another step. This is okay.

Here are the steps:

Step 1. The new food stays on another plate at dinnertime. When comfy with how it looks, go to step 2.

Step 2. All foods have their own smell. This is okay. Sniffing the new food helps the smell become familiar. When comfy with the new food's smell, go to step 3.

Step 3. Licking the new food tells a person about how the outside of the food feels and what it tastes like. When comfy with how the food feels and tastes on the outside, go to step 4.

Step 4. Step 4 is chewing and swallowing a very, very small amount of the new food. When people try a new food they usually try a very small piece first. Sometimes it helps to try a new food with a little ketchup on it. This is okay.

Following the four steps takes time. One step may take longer than another step. This is okay. Sometimes, even after time the new food may feel too uncomfy to try the next step. This is okay. I have discovered this information.

After step 4 I will have tried a new food. I may decide I like it. I may decide I dislike it. This is okay. I may make an important discovery and find another favourite food!

What is my underpants' job?

Mark was showing real distress when drops of urine wet his underpants. The distress caused him to insist on taking all clothing off and changing his entire set of clothes. At the time of this behaviour Mark was clean and dry and was not having 'accidents' with his toilet training. The drops of urine were happening at the end of urination and, although infrequent, this still meant we needed to bring a change of clothes for him everywhere we went. Although this was feasible when he was a small child, it was clear that this would be impossible to manage when he grew older. It would become an extremely restrictive behaviour for him and the family. I knew a Social Story™ would help.

The most important part of writing a Social Story™ is the gathering of information prior to writing. This allows the author to identify what information the child may be missing so that it can be shared with them in the Story. So to gather information I watched first hand the situation play out and noted exactly how, when and where it took place. I was able to note that Mark was able to tolerate drops of water on his vest, t-shirt, trousers and socks at other times without having to change. I talked to nursery school staff, who confirmed that the same was happening there.

To try and determine what the specific topic of the Story should be I sat down with Mark at a quiet calm time and we drew pictures in a Comic Strip Conversation (Gray, 1994) about what happened. He told me emphatically that underpants 'must be dry'. He seemed to believe that this was mandatory. Although this was never part of my toilet training talk I imagined perhaps he had heard it at nursery school or elsewhere. I explained an alternative view – that actually it was the underpants' job to keep the trousers dry and to do this job they needed to be able to soak up drops of 'wee' and dry out quickly. Mark's eyes opened wide with realisation. I said I would write a Social Story™ about it to help him. Several drafts of the Story were produced focusing on the topic that the underpants' job is to soak up the urine and protect the trousers. I made my statements about who wears them literally accurate with 'Many people…' mindful of the fact that inevitably one child at nursery might forget!

Illustrations followed the genre that Mark understood and had already responded to well. He was comfortable with my drawings that represented him and me. I used the colour red in the underpants because this was the colour underpants we used for our practical experiment on the drying out ability of underpants! If I was writing this Story for a child who was very colour literal I would use photographs in black and white, or, if the drawings were meaningful to him, I would include them in black and white.

I practised this experiment before I showed him so that I was sure it would work within the time limit I had set. I put the heating on as high as it would go and dropped three drops of water onto the underpants from a dropper, then placed them on the radiator and watched them dry out over five minutes. The choice of red colour allowed the wet area to be seen clearly and the change from the dark red shade to a paler red shade as it dried was obvious. It worked beautifully.

I read the Story to him every day for a week, by the end of which he would fill in the blanks of a partial sentence: 'It is the underpants'____ to soak up drops of wee'.

The behaviour stopped immediately after the first reading, and there never has been any need to reintroduce it again, although the Story remained in his Story box in his room, just in case. Occasionally over the ensuing weeks we would ask him what the underpants' job was as a reminder and he would smile and answer with glee.

This format of the Story referring to the purpose or job of an inanimate object has been used for other children who had difficulties around wearing outdoor shoes or coats with success. These Stories were individually researched before using this format to make sure it was this lack of information that was actually required by the child.

The immediate success of this Story was really life changing for me as a parent – I no longer had to pack and carry changes of clothes wherever we went. I was now absolutely hooked on this wonderful strategy! I had confidence that whenever an unusual response presented itself I would be able to unravel the missing information and share it with Mark in a Social Story™.

What is my underpants' job?

Many people wear underpants under their trousers, shorts, skirt or dress.

Many people wear a clean pair every day.

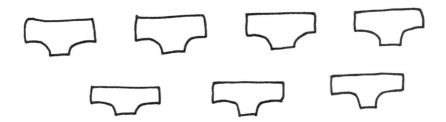

Underpants are usually made out of cloth that dries very quickly. It is the underpants' job to soak up drops of wee.

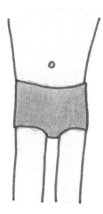

Underpants protect the trousers, shorts, dress or skirt from drops of wee. Sometimes drops of wee get on underpants. This is okay. Small drops of wee dry out quickly.

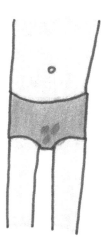

If drops of wee get on my underpants I will try to stay calm and wait for the underpants to do their job.

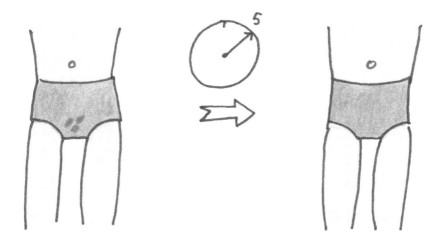

Mum will be pleased with me if I try to stay calm while the underpants do their job.

Stories about toileting
Where is the best place to put a wrapper?
What is poo?
I am learning to poo in a toilet

These next three Social Stories™ relate to toileting issues. This topic is vast and varied and each child will have his or her own individual issues to address. Some children are frightened of the seat and falling into the toilet, some are scared of the flush, others frightened to let go of the poo as part of themselves. Several children, however, responded well to an explanation of what poo is and why they should 'let go' of it, and also why the toilet is the best place to put poo. Although I did not specifically write them for my son, the following Stories used the ideas that worked for him around toilet training and have worked for others, so I believe they may be helpful in this collection. It is important to note that there is no need to reference poo as 'dirty' and no mention is made of the behaviour that focused the topic of the Story. The result is a factual exchange of missing information that makes letting go of poo into a toilet a logical and sensible action to take.

The first Story really is background work, describing how paper and plastic wrappers are rubbish and not edible or useful so we throw them away. It establishes that there is a correct place to put wrappers or rubbish, namely the bin. It is a starting place to explore dealing with unwanted things that leads to the idea that in a similar way the body throws away the rubbish left over from the food we have eaten, as poo, and the best place to put it is in the toilet. We are helping our body get rid of its rubbish! The second Story explains that poo has a strong smell from the rubbish it contains. It goes on to explain that because the water in the toilet washes it away in a flush, this keeps the toilet clean and smelling good, establishing a reason to poo in the toilet (rather than in the bin) and a purpose to the flush. Many children with autism become fascinated with the sewerage system, needing to know what happens when the poo goes down the pipes and this can be addressed in another Story if required.

Where is the best place to put a wrapper?

My name is .... I like to eat KitKats®. A KitKat® is a chocolate bar with a plastic wrapper on the outside.

When I have eaten all the chocolate bar I usually throw away the wrapper because I cannot eat the plastic wrapper. The wrapper is not useful for me. Many people call the wrapper 'rubbish' because it is not useful.

The best place for a plastic wrapper is in the bin. I usually put the KitKat® wrapper in the bin.

What is poo?

My name is ....

My favourite food is ....

I usually eat food at breakfast time, dinner time and lunch time. Sometimes I eat food at snack times too.

My body uses most of the food I eat for energy and making me grow.

The bits of food that the body cannot use are made into poo. Poo is the rubbish left after all the good stuff is used up in the body. The body gets rid of its rubbish by pushing poo out of the body through the bottom. This makes space in the body for more good food.

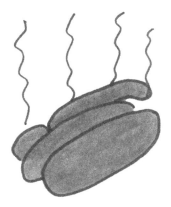

Poo has a strong smell. The smell comes from the rubbish in the poo.

Many people poo into a toilet. A toilet's job is to take the poo and its smell away safely by a big swoosh of water called a flush.

The flush washes the poo away down the toilet pipes and into the sewerage system. The sewerage system cleans the water. This is why toilets are the best place to poo.

Little children poo into a nappy. As children get older they learn to poo into a toilet. Many people poo into toilets. I am learning to poo into a toilet too.

I am learning to poo in a toilet

I am learning to poo in a toilet. When I need to poo here is what to do:

Step 1. Go into the toilet room. Lift the lid up on the toilet.

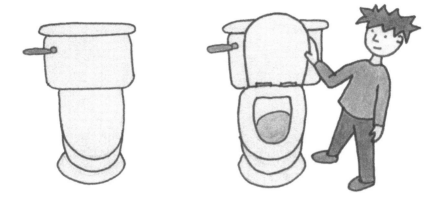

Step 2. Pull down trousers and underpants.

Step 3. Sit on the toilet seat and poo into the toilet.

Step 4. When the poo is finished take three pieces of toilet paper.

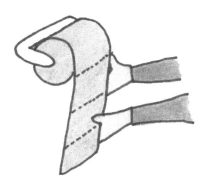

Step 5. Wipe bottom with toilet paper to clean where the poo came out. It's okay to take three more pieces of toilet paper if I need more.

Step 6. Put the used toilet paper in the toilet.

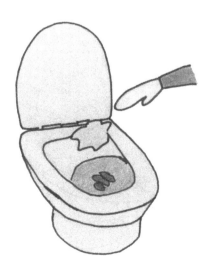

Step 7. Stand up.

Step 8. Pull up underpants and trousers.

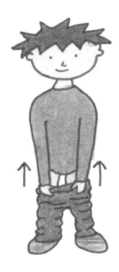

Step 9. Flush the toilet. The flush usually makes a whoosh sound. This is the water. The water takes the poo away.

Step 10. Wash hands and dry hands.

I am learning to poo in a toilet.

What job does my nose do?

Prior to writing every Social Story™ it is absolutely critical to put time and effort into information gathering around the target situation. The author needs to observe the situation several times on different days and, whilst observing, ask themselves what their young person might be experiencing in this situation, and how they may be perceiving it differently to the author. 'What information do I have in this situation that allows me to understand this social rule and other people's expectation or reaction?' is the question I ask myself when observing the child's response.

Like many young children Mark occasionally picked his nose and ate it. Initially I assumed that he was missing information about how uncomfortable this behaviour made other people feel. So I wrote a Social Story™ explaining other people's perspectives of the activity. The Story went on to explain that others like to be around people who keep them comfortable and that keeping others comfortable was a friendly thing to do. This Story took a week to write and illustrate, with many drafts to ensure it adhered to all the Social Story™ criteria. I was very pleased with it and was quietly confident that it would help.

However, when I read it with Mark it had absolutely no effect on the behaviour. Disappointed, I returned to examine the most critical step of information gathering. What had I missed? On reflection I realised I had made an assumption about the information Mark needed, based on what I knew about the autistic perspective, but had omitted to explore his reasons with him. As he was now talking and quite able to tell me, this was obviously an error.

Writing Social Stories™ to prepare a child for a new situation I usually make a 'best guess' about what might be difficult for that child and therefore what information they might need. I base my guess on what I know about how autism affects their perception, visiting the situation with my 'aspie-specs' on, and trying to imagine how this experience might feel for them.

Writing Stories, however, for a target situation where a child is displaying a response suggesting a difference in social understanding requires more information from the individual child, if possible, often in the form of a Comic Strip Conversation (Gray, 1994), a typed conversation on a computer or tablet (Faherty, 2014) or a side-by-side conversation during a relaxed time. When a child has little or no language, then the best guess method from careful observation is the best way forward.

When asked, Mark told me that the reason why children pick their nose and eat it is simple – 'it's a long time from breakfast to snack time'. Now that was a reason I would never have thought of!

With this information about the stimulus being hunger I could initially tackle the problem in a very practical way. I increased his breakfast and brought his snack time forwards. However, in social situations where he could not snack before a certain time the behaviour returned.

I needed to think carefully about why we neurotypicals are repulsed by anyone eating the contents of their nose. It is certainly not the texture alone – we eat slimy seafood after all –and it is not the salty taste – we eat a range of salty items. It must be an inherent understanding that it is 'dirty'. To find how I could explain this information I looked at a child's encyclopaedia on how the body works and there found a simple explanation of how the nose produces sticky stuff to trap dirt and germs in order to prevent them going into the body. This helps keep the body healthy (Hindley and King, 1995).

The following Story was written and read with Mark. I did not mention the target behaviour, just shared information on what the job of the nose was. After just one reading he came to his own conclusion, just like everyone else, that snot was not good to eat and the behaviour disappeared and did not return.

It is important to note here that for Mark it was clearly not a sensory issue of discomfort from the nose being full, or an aversion to the sensation of blowing the nose, although this may be the case for another child.

This Story taught me many things about Social Story™ writing, which is why it is included in this book. First, it taught me that a Story can be perfectly constructed according to all the Social Story™ criteria, with literally relevant and beautiful illustrations, and still not give the information required by that individual child. If it is not successful the conclusion may be made that for this child Social Stories™ don't work. This may be a faulty conclusion. A Social Story™ must be researched before writing to ensure that the author has identified, as much as is possible, what the information required is. There are no short cuts! It also reminded me of the many different avenues of research available for helpful information such as dictionaries, children's encyclopaedias and the Internet.

Second, this Story taught me that monitoring the Story and the effect it has on the child's response is crucial (Gray, 2010). When the Story was not making any difference to the response I quickly stopped and went back to the drawing board.

Third, that often there may be a practical solution, like more food! I have been asked in the past to write a Story for a child where, on observation, it was clearly a sensory stimulus that the child was responding to. When the stimulus was removed the response disappeared. It is important that sensory input in the situation is assessed as part of the observation prior to writing the Story. A Social Story™ is not always required!

What job does my nose do?

My name is Mark. This is a picture of my face.

In the middle of my face is my nose. I breathe through my nose and I smell through my nose.

My nose has another really important job. In the air around me there are very, very, very small bits of dirt, dust and germs. These are so small I cannot see them.

When I breathe in through my nose sometimes the dirt, dust and germs come into my nose with the air.

My nose makes special sticky stuff to trap these germs and dirt. This sticky stuff stops the germs and dirt going further into my body. This helps keep me healthy. Some people call this sticky stuff 'snot' or 'bogeys'.

When my nose has trapped lots of dirt and germs I may blow the sticky stuff out of my nose into a tissue. This is okay. This helps my nose get rid of the germs and dirt in the sticky stuff.

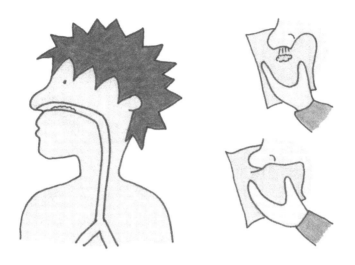

Then I may throw the tissue in the bin and wash my hands with soap and water.

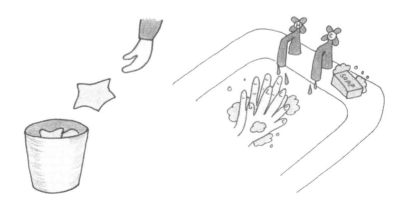

I will try to remember to blow my nose into a tissue, put the tissues in the bin and wash my hands. This will help my nose keep me healthy.

How to stay safe and comfy in a supermarket

Shopping at a supermarket can be a tiring and frustrating experience for a neurotypical adult even without children. For a child on the spectrum it can be an overwhelming, unpleasant and uncomfortable sensory experience, and a social nightmare!

A large percentage of children with autism are known to have sensory integration disorder resulting in hypo- or hypersensitivities to noise, light, smell and taste, as well as proprioceptive stimuli and touch. This may result in the child experiencing uncomfortable levels of incoming sensory stimuli and being unable to accommodate them so that they can reach a comfortable status quo.

In a supermarket there are strong overhead lights with bright visual displays, loudspeaker music and announcements, differing smells from the various counters and even different temperatures in different aisles. Coupled with this sensory overload there is queuing, involving the physical proximity of people in a crowded space, and waiting while a parent chooses products they want. It is no surprise that a child with autism finds this environment one of the most challenging.

To help Mark cope with supermarket shopping I needed to share some information about supermarkets with him in a Social Story™. I began my research by first walking through a supermarket, gathering information by observing the experience from my son's perspective. What sensory elements might be uncomfortable for him?

What social elements would he have understanding of, and what would he need some information about? What strategies could he use to make himself physically more comfortable in the context of the shop?

A Social Story™ on 'How to stay safe and comfy in a supermarket' was written addressing this information. It was implemented with the following supportive strategies.

I always tried to shop at quiet times and took Mark along only when I had a small amount to do. I would choose a small supermarket if I could and one where I would know where everything was likely to be, so that my visit would be quick. Each time on entering the store I would point out where Customer Services was in case he became separated from me. Because carrying something in his hand comforted him he would be allowed to carry a small car or toy. To reduce the glare of the overhead lighting, he would wear a peaked cap and sunglasses, and put his earphones in, not always attached to any music but just to reduce the external noise. I wanted him to be able to hear me if I called him.

To make it more interesting for him I would occasionally give him a very small list of shopping to do to help me. Initially it would have the labels of his favourite foods stuck on a piece of paper. Later on it would be the names of the familiar foods he liked. I would help him locate the aisle to begin with, and later would shadow him as he did it 'on his own'.

Knowing that the queuing at the checkout would be a difficult time for him (see also, 'Learning to queue at the checkout'), I would choose one that had a chair nearby where I could see him and he could see me. I brought a small bag of distractions called the 'checkout bag' for him to look at while I queued and paid. This was kept solely for shopping trips. I had a similar one saved for hospital appointments, a 'hospital bag', and also one for travelling, 'the delay bag'. As he got older and learned more about turn taking and queuing Mark was able to spend longer in the queue with me before going to the chair. Mark now can independently shop at a supermarket, but he always remembers to bring his earphones with him.

Social Stories™ are extremely effective at reducing anxiety in a child with autism who is about to try a new or challenging experience. The aim should be not only to share information with them so that they are able to have social understanding, but also to teach them to prepare themselves so that they are comfortable in a potentially hostile sensory experience.

How to stay safe and comfy in a supermarket

Sometimes Mum and I go to a supermarket to buy some shopping. A supermarket is a big shop that sells food and drink and lots of other things too. Tesco is a supermarket and Sainsbury's is another supermarket.

There are lots of different things to buy in a supermarket. Mum usually has a list of the things she needs to buy when we go to a supermarket. Sometimes Mum has a list for me too.

A supermarket may be a noisy place. There may be music playing. There may be announcements. There are usually bright lights so that people may see the things to buy on the shelves.

When I go to the supermarket I usually wear my cap and bring my earphones and sunglasses with me. These usually help keep me feel more comfy in the supermarket.

Sometimes I bring my Postman Pat van, sometimes I bring another toy. When we go shopping Mum usually brings my checkout bag too!

Usually there are lots of people shopping in a supermarket. Mum knows how to keep me safe when there are lots of people. It is easy to get separated from Mum when there are lots of people. Mum knows where I am when I hold her hand.

Sometimes Mum needs both hands to put the shopping in the trolley or to push the trolley. When Mum cannot hold my hand I may hold the edge of the trolley.

Customer Services is a safe place to go if I cannot see Mum. The adult there will call Mum to collect me.

Sometimes the shopping takes a short time, sometimes it takes a long time. When all the shopping is done it is paid for at a checkout. When the shopping is all paid for and packed into bags, Mum and I put the bags in the car and go home.

Learning to queue at the checkout

Sometimes Mum and I go to a supermarket
to buy some shopping. A supermarket is a
big shop that sells food and drink and lots
of other things too. Tesco is a supermarket
and Sainsbury's is another supermarket.
There are lots of different things to buy in a
supermarket.

Mum and I put the shopping in our shopping
trolley. When all the shopping is done it is paid
for at a checkout. The supermarket usually
has many checkouts. Only one person can be
served at a checkout at a time.

Taking turns is a fair way of sharing one thing that everyone cannot use at the same time. To take turns the people line up by a checkout with their shopping.

Sometimes the queue is short, sometimes the queue is long.

Waiting patiently in the checkout queue is an important skill to learn. Many people find it difficult to wait patiently at a checkout. I am learning to wait patiently at the checkout. When there is an empty seat near the checkout Mum will tell me to sit there.

Here are some things that may help me wait patiently while Mum pays for the shopping:

Playing with my games or toys from my checkout bag

Listening to my music with my earphones

Counting penguins

one penguin, two penguins, three penguins, four penguins....

Playing with my Game Boy®

Feeling my hanky in my pocket.

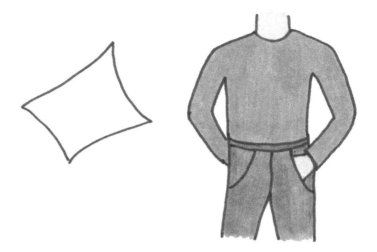

When the shopping is all paid for and packed into bags, Mum and I put the bags in the car and go home.

Why do babies cry?

In order to survive babies have to cry for attention, and human brains are wired to respond to that sound in preference to all others. A baby's cry will pierce our consciousness and arouse us from the deepest sleep. To a child with sensory integration difficulties this may be magnified and extremely uncomfortable. I believe this may be why it is a particular problem for those with autism. Sometimes it helps the child to know that there is a reason why the cry is so difficult to ignore and shut out – it is for the survival of the species!

Mark has always liked babies but finds their high-pitched cries very uncomfortable. A Social Story™ sharing information on the reasons for a baby's cry and a few strategies to keep him more comfortable were very helpful and effective.

A second Story, 'What to do when another child is crying', guiding him to seek help was useful because not only was he informing a responsible adult, who may be able to help the child and stop the crying, but also in moving away from the immediate vicinity of the crying to find help he was making himself more comfortable.

Sharing information on who would be best to help the baby or child is also important to prevent the child with autism attempting to do it himself, which may be alarming for the parent or carer of the child.

This Story has been adapted and used successfully for other children. I have not included illustrations for the second Story.

Why do babies cry?

Babies need help to look after themselves. Usually a baby has a special grown up who looks after them. The grown up may be a dad, a mum or someone else. Because the grown up knows the baby well they are the best person to help the baby.

When babies are born they cannot talk. When babies are hungry, thirsty or uncomfy they cry. Babies cry so that their grown up will come and help them feel better. Crying is the only way the baby can ask for help. This is okay. This is what babies do.

A baby's cry is made to be loud and difficult to ignore so that their grown up will come and help.

Little by little, as they grow babies learn to talk and tell their grown up when they need help. As they learn to talk babies need to cry less often.

Sometimes when a baby cries their grown up makes them better straight away and then the crying stops quickly. Sometimes it takes time for a grown up to work out what the baby needs and he or she may cry for a longer time.

When a baby cries I may use my headphones/earphones until the crying stops. Using my headphones/earphones will usually make the crying quieter.

I will try to remember that the crying will stop when the baby feels better. Mummy will be pleased with me.

What to do when another child is crying

Sometimes when a child is hurt or upset they cry. Usually this is because it has happened suddenly and the child is shocked. Many times when a grown up comes the child starts to feel better and stops crying quickly.

A child's cry is made to be loud so that a grown up will come to help. This is why it is difficult to ignore. Sometimes when another child cries it may be uncomfy for my ears.

When a child is crying, I may ask them if they need a grown up. If they say yes I may tell a grown up that someone needs help. This is a kind and friendly thing to do. Other children like boys who are kind and friendly.

Using my headphones/earphones will usually make the crying quieter. I will work on staying calm. Here are two things that may help me stay calm:

Feeling my hanky in my pocket.

Counting to 10 penguins.

I am learning what to do when another child is crying.

How to stay safe around wasps

This Social Story™ was written initially for Mark about bees. The Story was then later adapted successfully for a child with autism who was having problems going out and about in the summer because of a fear of wasps.

Although fear of buzzing insects is a common fear amongst the neurotypical population I have noticed that many children with autism have huge difficulty in staying calm around an unpredictable insect such as a bee or wasp, and frequently parents ask me if Social Stories™ can help.

Sometimes the fear comes from a common misunderstanding that the wasp or bee is specifically chasing the child in order to sting him. The unpredictable nature of the flight of a bee or wasp is deeply unsettling, and the buzzing, particularly if there is a hypersensitivity to noise, may also be very alarming. One child told me that the 'angry' bee was chasing him. This concept of 'angry' came from someone describing the buzzing in this way, and was central to his individual concern.

Before writing a Story I needed to do some research. I discovered that bees and wasps moved from place to place quickly, not to chase, but because they were trying to decide where to land. They both have a very acute sense of smell that helps them identify flowers and sweet things to eat. On their antennae they have over 100 odour receptors! So they are continually smelling the air trying to locate sweet smells. This is helpful information because it means they will be attracted to a person who has a sweet smell on them.

Bees are also able to detect the movement of air particles around them using specific sensors on their antennae and this may explain their response to a person swatting at them with hands or other items. Staying as still as possible or moving slowly near a wasp or bee is therefore sensible and less likely to cause them to feel under threat.

A bee may flap its wings more than 230 times a second just to hover, and this makes the distinctive buzzing sound. Because of the large amounts of energy that bees and wasps use up flying around they require high energy sugary food. This is available to them in plant nectar and pollen in spring and early summer, and later on in fruit and late flowering plants. Another source is in outdoor sweet food and drinks served or spilled by humans in the garden!

During my research I was also delighted to discover there are several insect repellants on the market that specifically will repel wasps and bees. Some are even contained within a children's sunscreen.

I decided that all this information would be helpful in alleviating some of the fears of bees and wasps that had arisen from misunderstandings of their behaviour! I needed to share the perspective of the stinging insect with the child. For each individual child, time was also taken to try and find out the specific information they might need, using observation and drawing conversations. There is obviously a lot of scope here to add numerical data and scientific facts for a child who is interested in this and understands it.

I wrote two Stories titled 'How to stay safe around wasps' and 'How do I move safely near a wasp?' To practically and concretely support the first Story I had a t-shirt recently stained with sweet-smelling ice lolly drips, and a bottle of insect repellant so the child could smell the sweetness and also clearly see and hold the repellant.

These Stories were successful not only for the child it was written for, but also for another neurotypical family member who was frightened of wasps. However, the little boy did insist on wearing wasp repellant every day so another Story had to be written describing the life cycle of a wasp, so that he understood that repellant was only necessary in the spring/summer months.

For Mark the fear was more deep seated as it was based on a painful sting experience and, although the Story definitely helped, resulting in him finally allowing his bedroom window to be open in warm weather, it has taken a longer time for him to become less panicked in their presence – another slow burner!

How to stay safe around wasps

Knowing some facts about wasps may help children keep safe around them.

Wasps are insects. They fly around when the weather is warm.

The buzzing noise comes from their wings moving up and down very, very quickly. Wasps move from place to place deciding where to go.

Wasps like sweet foods. Wasps like the smell that sweet foods make. While they are moving they are smelling for sweet smells. Wasps like to land on sweet food and eat it.

Sometimes they like to land on people who have sweet smells on their hands or face or neck. This happens when someone has eaten something sweet like a lolly or a piece of fruit or drink.

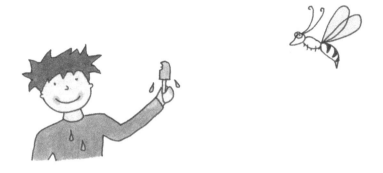

Usually, washing the hands and face after eating sweet things takes away the sweet smell. Sometimes eating indoors with the windows closed can keep the sweet smell away from wasps.

Another way of keeping wasps away is to spray on a smell that wasps dislike. Insect repellant is a special spray that is sprayed on hands, feet, arms and neck. The spray makes a smell the wasps dislike. The wasps usually move away from the smell.

An adult knows the right amount of insect repellant to use. An adult may help me put insect repellant on. When wasps smell insect repellant they will usually try to move away from the smell.

I will try to wash my hands and face after eating sweet foods and to use insect repellant in the summer. I am learning to stay safe around wasps.

How do I move safely near a wasp?

I am learning how to be safe near a wasp. Knowing some things about wasps helps me move safely near a wasp.

A wasp can detect movement of air. When a wasp is in still air it feels calm. A calm wasp is a safe wasp. Moving slowly or standing still keeps the air around me still.

Moving quickly or moving the air with my hands makes the air move quickly around me. Air moving quickly nearby may make the wasp frightened. A frightened wasp may sting to defend itself.

The safe way to move near a wasp is calmly and slowly. I will try to work on moving slowly or standing still around wasps.

I am learning to move safely near a wasp.

Sharing the diagnosis with a Social Story™
What are worries?

Every child is unique. Every child with autism is unique. Every child with or without autism is also part of a unique family. So the decision of how and when to tell a child his diagnosis must be an individual choice that fits the individual child.

I know the decision of when and how to share a diagnosis of autism with a child always weighs heavily on a parent's heart. I am sharing here the way I did it with a Social Story™, mindful that many have asked me for advice about how I went about it. It may not be suitable for your child, and how you decide to go about it should be entirely your choice led by your child's needs.

I told Mark about his diagnosis in a quiet gradual manner that allowed him to acquire the knowledge in a way that I hoped he would be able to deal with positively. I worked continually hard to keep his self-esteem positive with a 'Happy' book full of positive achievements, comments and happy times. I always emphasised his many strengths when confronted with his difficulties in order to give him positive perspective.

I then introduced the concept of worries. We all have worries. Worries are carried inside us and others cannot see them or know about them unless we choose to share them. Worries can seem less once shared with someone we trust and can be helped by others.

I gave him examples of all our different worries within the family and then explored some things that we do to help with our worries.

Whenever he presented with a difficulty that was causing him concern I described it as a worry and then looked for a solution. Mark became used to a solution being possible for most worries, whatever their cause, and if not a solution an improvement in most cases. I used the term 'Mark's Worries' when discussing his autism with professionals in his presence so they knew what we were calling his autism and also to give Mark a feeling of a continued understanding of his problems.

It was fortunate that at the time 'Pokemon®' games and trading cards were popular amongst Mark's peers and in trying to encourage friendship skills we had introduced Mark to the world of Pokemon®, which he took to with relish. Pokemon® are Japanese animated fictional creatures who battle each other by pitting their strengths against each other. Each Pokemon® has a weakness that makes it vulnerable in particular situations, much like children with autism, and they need to use their strengths to overcome it. This interest allowed exploration of strengths and weaknesses with Mark and led to a few very effective Social Stories™ illustrated with Pokemon®. Talking in Pokemon® language seemed to be a comfortable place for him. Interestingly Pokemon® was devised by a Japanese games designer, Satoshi Tajiri, who some believe was on the autistic spectrum.

As time went on Mark gradually became more aware of his difference from others and how his worries were sometimes more complex than others. We acknowledged his growing understanding, never brushing his worries off as insignificant, and decided to tell him the name of his worries in a matter of fact fashion in much the same way you would name a group of similar articles, for example 'stationery' is the name for a collection of paper, card, pencils, etc.

I wrote a Social Story™ about the topic and rehearsed what I would say and how I would say it so I would be ready when the moment was right. I made the Story relevant to Mark's worries and his interests, and this may make it unsuitable for another child without suitable adaptation. I was influenced by a Social Story™ workbook from Carol Gray's template 'Pictures of me' (Gray Center, 2005), which explores a child's personality and talents, as well as his diagnosis, in order to safeguard self-esteem.

Ideally I wanted to tell him before he became adolescent as I knew that insecurities about fitting in may be more acute then. The ever-present threat that someone else might tell him in a negative way was a constant worry. The other influencing concern I had was a fear that Mark might give up trying to improve some skills designating them 'autistic' and beyond his control once given the label of autism.

Eventually the time to tell him was sprung upon us by the imminent publication of his name and diagnosis in the local paper in an article recognising the fantastic commitment and achievement of his learning support assistant, Helen Barker, who had guided him through the last ten years of school. So on the way to school in the car after talking about how much his worries over games lessons at school had improved, I popped in that his worries had a name.

'You know how we talk about your worries? Did you know that there is a name for them? It's called autism. And you know what – other people have autism and have similar worries to you.'

His response was 'Oh okay!' I told him I had written a Social Story™ about it, which we read the following afternoon together.

Sharing his diagnosis opened the door for many subsequent questions; for example, 'Is it my autism that makes this difficult for me?' On nearly every occasion I was able to tell him that, although autism presented some challenges, it also brought some unusual and useful skills. For example, he was aware that others were not disturbed by a dead pixel on a screen, and many could not even see it, whereas for him it caused such distress that he could not continue to use the screen. I was able to show him that, although this was a sometimes difficult aspect of autism, it also was a potential strength and may lead to a job in the detection of faulty screens in the future.

Because Mark considered Social Stories™ already as a remedy or a solution, providing the information he needed to help his worries, he was reassured not frightened by his diagnosis. I am so very grateful for that, Carol!

I have included this Story in this first book and not in the second, because I believe the groundwork for it needs to be established during those early years before the diagnosis is shared later on.

What are worries?

A worry is a thought or feeling that makes a person feel unsettled or uncomfy. Many people have worries. Worries are carried inside a person and cannot be seen by other people.

I have a special tool box to help me with my worries. Social Stories™ help me too. Many of my worries are helped when I tell my Mum or Mrs B and we find a solution together.

Sometimes people's worries may be very similar and the person may be described as 'belonging' to a group of people who have the same worries. People with worries similar to mine belong to a group of people who have autism.

People with autism may have worries when things change unexpectedly.

People with autism may have worries about making and keeping friendships. Many people with autism have worries about understanding what other people mean when they talk. Just like me!

People who have autism are also often intelligent, loyal, honest and brave. People with autism have many talents – just like me! There are also many many famous people who may have had autism, for example, great musicians like Amadeus Mozart,

great scientists like Albert Einstein,

amazing inventors like Bill Gates

and awesome game designers like Satoshi Tajiri.

Belonging to a group of people who share a worry may be a comforting thing. Sometimes it may be good to know that others feel the same. I am not the only one with these worries.

I also belong to many groups of people apart from the autism group. Here are all the groups I belong to:

A person may choose to tell someone he trusts what his worries are. I may choose to tell someone I trust about my autism worries. Mum, Dad, my brothers and Mrs B know about my autism worries. All of these people will try to help me if I ask them to.

I belong to a group of people who share the worries and talents of autism and I belong to many, many other groups of people too!

A Story for parents at L.A.S.T.!

During my time co-running a support group for parents I have heard about, and witnessed, many discussions between a parent and professionals around a child's challenging responses. I have noted that a defensive stance, although the most natural response of a parent, is seldom effective in finding a solution, and frequently results in a breakdown in the relationship between the parent and the professional. Breakdowns in this relationship are counterproductive and not in our children's best interests or our own.

Looking for a positive strategy for parents in our support group for these situations, I combined the guidelines for active listening with a communicative method of response rather than a defensive one (Siegel and Silverstein, 2001) to develop an effective way forward, mindful of the need to keep a productive positive relationship with the professional. The strategy involves bringing to mind an acronym L.A.S.T., which will be explained below. A Social Story™ for parents was also written to support it!

In order to be able to resolve a confrontational situation we need the person talking to us to be willing to compromise with us. We need that person to feel that we have really listened to their concerns and have taken them on board even if we disagree with them. If we don't listen, the conversation becomes a 'getting my bit in' with neither party listening to the other. So when we talk to someone we need to *listen* to them fully. We need to let them say everything they planned to. Even if we don't agree we should let them finish. This is good listening and respectful. During this time we should try to look and be interested and engaged with what they are saying.

Once they have finished, we should try to repeat back to them in our own words the message we think they are trying to get across, for example 'That must have been very difficult to handle on a school trip. You must feel very frustrated.' We call this *acknowledging* what they have said. If we are accurate in what we say, and we have rightly identified what they are feeling, saying it out loud back to them will immediately make them feel validated, understood and calmer.

We then can suggest ways to *solve it together*. 'Can we work together to discover what caused this behaviour? I can share some things that help calm him at home when this happens?'

This simple sequence of listening, acknowledging and solving together is not easy to do and takes some practice. Each step is difficult and each is important, so we need to remember them as one following the other. Only together will they make an improvement in the effectiveness of our communication. The acronym L.A.S.T. may help us remember that if we want our relationship with this person to last we need to be mindful of L.A.S.T. So here is the Social Story™ summarising this strategy for parents – at last!

Learning to solve problems together with professionals

Mums and Dads love their children. When a child is having a difficulty, parents want to help solve it. This is a natural and normal thing for a Mum or Dad to want to do.

Sometimes a child responds to a situation in a way that is difficult for others to understand. When faced with a complaint about a child's response a parent usually tries to explain the reasons behind the response in an attempt to help others understand.

Sometimes parents may need to *listen* and then *acknowledge* how difficult the situation may have been for that person, validating their feelings. Once listened to, and their point of view acknowledged, many people are ready to listen to and learn from the parent finding *solutions together*.

I will try and remember to listen and acknowledge so that we can solve together. Thinking about L.A.S.T. may help me remember.

A Story for siblings

The following Story is not a Social Story™. Nevertheless it is still an important and successful story and I believe deserves a special mention for parents beginning their family's journey with autism because being aware of this topic early on can save many problems arising later with siblings.

One of the most enduring yet potentially damaging emotions humans experience is sibling rivalry. We only need to look at adult relationships to see problems still present within those who feel that they were less appreciated by their parents in favour of a sibling. Equally sibling rivalry can stimulate us to take on new challenges, develop our skills to overcome difficulties and refine our compassionate and caring natures.

As parents of children with autism our strongest desire is to bring up all our children in a nurturing happy home, encouraging each sibling to fulfil his own potential. We hope that in the future siblings would have a caring concern for their brother or sister, not out of duty, but out of love. We want his or her relationship with each sibling to be a positive one and to last a lifetime.

We encourage our children to help and care for their sibling, but in doing so we may be positively reinforcing caring behaviour to the exclusion of normal childlike behaviour, without ever being aware that we are doing so. How often do we ask them to keep an eye on their brother and, without meaning to, discourage expression of feelings of jealousy and resentment by dismissing them with explanations of autism?

Some children may reach adulthood with an unresolved resentment of the difficulties imposed on them by growing up with their sibling with autism. Others, unable to express their emotions, may act them out by withdrawing, becoming mini-parents, acting up or trying to super-achieve. Of course many children will learn positive caring skills and this is reflected in the high proportion of siblings choosing caring careers. How can we as parents encourage our children to deal with their childhood experience in a positive way?

First, we need to know how they are dealing with the many different emotions they are experiencing on a day-to-day basis. We will only know how they feel if we make time to listen. Here the L.A.S.T. strategy mentioned in the previous Story comes into play again for siblings. Our child needs to be able to express his feelings without anxiety that we will be upset, angry or dismissive. We need to listen, listen and listen! A regular labelled private time with uninterrupted space with him to talk, or not, depending on how he feels, will give him the opportunity he needs.

Once listened to, the feelings expressed need to be acknowledged as being valid and normal feelings to have. Often saying something like 'I guess that must make you feel really mad, I think it is a normal way to feel in that situation' will acknowledge his feeling and validate it.

The difficulty the child has in dealing with the feeling is resolved when it can be freely expressed, without negative feedback, learning that it is normal to have these feelings and that we understand. Talking together about ways to manage a situation so that the sibling's feelings are considered can then often resolve the situation. 'Let's work out some way to manage it' can dissipate guilt felt for feeling angry. Our child may have some good ideas already or we may be able to suggest some, for example 'How about you have your friends over next Friday while Dad takes your sister to the zoo?'

Siblings, once listened to and their point of view acknowledged, are usually happy to try and solve problems together with the parent. Other more senior family members expressing an opinion about our child's response also respond much more favourably once listened to, their feelings acknowledged. All are then much more ready to find a solution with the parent.

The acronym L.A.S.T., which stands for 'Listening, Acknowledging and Solving Together' helps us remember that if we want the relationship between the child and his sibling with autism to last, or the relationship between a family member and ourselves to last, we need to be mindful of L.A.S.T.!

Implementing L.A.S.T. alone of course is not always enough to reassure young children of their unassailable right to our love. Sometimes, explaining abstract concepts in a concrete permanent and visual way helps. Recognising that my neurotypical sons needed to understand how much I loved each one of them I wrote the following story for them. They were used to seeing me write Stories for Mark so it was important that they had one too on this important topic. Both had their own copy to keep. This is not a Social Story™ but it is definitely a love story!

Many parents I have shared this love story with have put it in place in their own homes with several feeding back that it had positive results for them too. One talented mother made a heart out of padded material which contained equal 'love sections' that could be removed to see their equality and then replaced. This worked well for her children! I hope that any parents reading this will find it helpful too.

My dear ......,

My heart is divided into sections, one section for each one of my family. Each one of you has an equal section of my heart and it is filled with love. It is absolutely forever yours. Nothing can change your section. No one else can take away any part of your section, nor can you increase it in any way. You are my son and I am your mum. There is nothing you can do in this life that will change that. You do not need to defend your section of my heart and my love for you, it is always there safe for you. You can relax.

Love Mum

References

Attwood, T. (2008) *The Complete Guide to Asperger Syndrome*. London: Jessica Kingsley Publishers.

Bowler, D.M., Gardiner, J.M. and Grice, S. J. (2000) 'Episodic memory and remembering in adults with Asperger syndrome.' *Journal of Autism and Developmental Disorders 30,* 4, 295–304.

Faherty, C. (2014) *Autism... What Does It Mean To Me?* 2nd edition. Arlington, VA: Future Horizons.

Gray, C. (1994) *Comic Strip Conversations*. Arlington, VA: Future Horizons.

Gray, C. (2010) *The New Social Story™ Book, 10th Anniversary edition*. Arlington, VA: Future Horizons.

Gray, C. (2014) *Story Master*. Training Resource.

Gray, C. (2015) *The New Social Story™ Book, 15th Anniversary edition*. Arlington, VA: Future Horizons.

Gray Center for Social Learning and Understanding (2005) 'Pictures of me.' *Social Stories™ Quarterly 1,* 1, 14–25.

Hindley, J. and King, C. (1995) *How Your Body Works*. London: Usborne.

Howley, M. and Arnold, E. (2005) *Revealing the Hidden Social Code*. London: Jessica Kingsley Publishers.

Meiner, C. (2003) *Share and Take Turns*. Minneapolis, MN: Free Spirit Publishing.

Siegel, B and Silverstein, S. (2001) *What About Me ? Growing Up with a Developmentally Disabled Sibling*. Boston, MA: Perseus.

Vermeulen, P. (2012) *Autism as Context Blindness*. Lenexa, KN: AAPC.

Index

achievements 28–9, 86, 126, 193
Arnold, E. 86
Attwood, T. 35, 38
autism 17, 21
   child's perspective 22, 23–5, 154
   clothing problems 134–6
   diagnosis 193–6
   eye contact 51–2
   fear of buzzing insects 182
   identifying emotional states 35
   insincere thanks 111–12
   learning good manners 91
   learning social eating skills 95–7
   negative commands 25–6
   sensory issues 118–19, 126
   supermarket shopping 161

babies 175
Barker, Helen 17, 28, 195
bees 182–4
bereavement 30
body language 23
Bowler, D.M. 29

calmness 35
   achieving calmness 35–6
   chill out time 37–8
   fear of bees and wasps 182–4
   neurotypical perspective 38–9
   soothing strategies 37
   special interests 37
central coherence 23
chill out time 37–8

Comic Strip Conversations 19, 79,
   111, 134
context sensitivity 23, 25
   different meanings of 'excuse me'
     102–3
conversation skills 78–80
   interrupting conversation 85–6
   interrupting telephone conversation
     86

disappointments 111–12

eating together 95–7
emotions 35
   calmness 35–9
   sibling rivalry 207–9
excuse me 102–4
experiences 29–30
   positive experiences 28–9
eye contact 51–2, 79

facial expressions 23, 52, 78
fairness 24–5
   taking turns 66–7
food preferences 29
   eating out 96–7
   finding another favourite food
     126–8
Future Horizons 17

games 79, 97, 194
Gardiner, J.M. 29
Gray Center 195

Gray, C. 17, 19, 21, 27, 29, 38, 52, 61, 79, 85, 111, 126, 134, 155, 196
Grice, S.J. 29

hand dryers 118–19
Hindley, J. 155
Howley, M. 86

information processing 22–3
interests, special 37, 78–9, 194

kind words 61–3
King, C. 155

L.A.S.T. (listening, acknowledging, solving it together) 204–5, 209
language 25–6, 27, 154

language acquisition 56, 61, 78, 103–4

learning kind words 61–3

Pokemon® language 194
letters, thank you 111–12
listening skills 51–2
    conversation 78–80
    listening to siblings 208–9
    parents and professionals 204–5

manners 91
    table manners 95–7
Market Field Special School, Essex 21
MAZE 21
Meiner, C. 66

negative commands 25–6
neurotypical perspective 22–3, 24, 25–6, 154
    eye contact 51–2
    writing Social Stories™ 38–9
nose-blowing 155
nose-picking 153–4
    discouraging 154–6

parents' support 204–5
please and thank you 91
Pokemon® 194
poo and pooing 140–1
positive experiences 28–9
positive language 26, 27
presents 111–12
professionals 204–5
puberty 29

queueing 66, 67, 162–63

rubbish disposal 140–1

self-esteem 20, 26, 86, 193, 195
self-reflection 28–9
    finding another favourite food 126–8
sensory issues 118–19, 126
    crying babies 175
    identifying 155–6
    supermarkets 161–2
sharing 66–7
    eating together 95–7
    sharing social information 26–7
shopping 161–2
siblings 207–9
situation change 23–4
Social Articles 17, 103, 104
social eating 95
Social Stories™ 17–21
    criteria 27
    help with context blindness 102–3
    remembering child's perspective 38–9
    self-reflection 29
    sharing social information 26–7
Social Understanding 17, 20–1
soothing strategies 37, 38
Spectrum, Colchester, Essex 20–1
supermarket shopping 161–2
    supportive strategies 162–63

table manners 95–7
Tajiri, Satoshi 194

taking turns 66-7
telephone calls 86
thank you 91

thank you letters 111–12
theory of mind 24, 25, 61, 111
Timmins, Mark 17–20
  coping with autism diagnosis
    194–6
  coping with disappointment
    111–12
  finding another favourite food
    126–8
  growing up 28–30
  learning kind words 61–3
  learning to be calm 35–9
  overcoming fear of hand dryers
    118–19
toileting issues 140–1

underpants 134–6

Vermeulen, P. 22, 102
voice, tone of 23, 25, 35, 52

waiting skills 56–7
  interrupting conversation 85–6
  queuing at a checkout 162–63
  social eating 96–7
wasps 182–4
waste disposal 140–1
worries 193
  looking for solutions 194